Leslie Dean has written another great book about life's trauma. She has given us an insight into the struggles within family and people we associate with. It shows that the soul, while suppressed by dominating people can still find the light and hope. It delivers a view of how people being controlled can also have an effect on the other member of the family. Some may or may not believe that angels occur in our life through people who appear at our lowest times, but it reaffirms the faith the author has. I highly recommend this book as delivering a solid story of life's emotional struggles.

Pugsley
Barnes and Noble review

THE RESCUE OF AN

. . . the final chapter

Leslie T. Dean

www.innovativeinkpublishing.com
Send all inquiries to:
4050 Westmark Drive
Dubuque, IA 52004-1840

Dedication

This book is dedicated to all of those who have experienced the painful
aftermath of intergenerational trauma.
Be encouraged.
He has kept track of all your sorrows and collected all your tears in His bottle.
For they are precious to Him.
And He will return to you all the enemy has stolen.
He will not leave you as an orphan.
He will come to you . . .

"The Rescue of an Orphan" was a captivating continuation of Leslie's journey and her deep longing for love and happiness. I was unable to put it down! This second part of her life story, Leslie bravely shares the emotional and often chaotic decisions that shaped her life, and sometimes the result was heartbreaking. The way God led Leslie to see the Truth of His love for her was miraculous! Her story beautifully reveals God's love in the darkest of circumstances.

Don't miss this book series, or you will miss an opportunity to be inspired!

—Robin Smith, *BA Family Studies NCAA Certified Pastoral Counselor AACC Certified Life and Trauma Coach*

In her sequel to *The Making of an Orphan*, Dean bravely invites readers in . . . into her painful choices and missed opportunities. Into betrayals and heartache. Not just once but over and over. The ups and downs of her adult life exemplify the pervasiveness of unaddressed intergenerational trauma. Dean writes with a rare vulnerability that engages readers' intrigue, weaving in therapeutic insights that lance open the inner workings that drove her.

Maybe you can find yourself in the pages of *The Rescue of an Orphan* like I did and identify with one—or the myriad—of the scenarios that unfold. But hold on tight, because she's not just going to show you her side of the story; she's going to show you the fingerprints of her Rescuer . . . and take you through the journey of discovering if a life lived in the wake of abandonment, rejection, and oppression could really be made new again.

—Colleen Morris, *Master of Arts in English*

Leslie Dean is a gifted writer! Once you start reading one of her books, you don't want to put it down! I am grateful for her courage to share her story. I highly recommend her previous books, *Forgiven Much* as well as *The Making of an Orphan*, and now her latest masterpiece. . . *The Rescue of an Orphan*!

God truly has rescued her, and her books will inspire you to trust God at a deeper level. This book, along with her others, captures well God's heart for redemption! Like Leslie, each one of us has a story, and often "our story" contains much pain. But God wants us to find Him in the midst of that pain and allow

Him to turn what the enemy meant for evil into good. He is the redeemer of all things, and He will one day redeem ALL things unto himself.

Dawn Robyn, *White Sulphur Springs*

In this sequel to *The Making of an Orphan*, Leslie Dean has once again shown vulnerability in sharing very personal stories as she relates the continuing impact of intergenerational trauma. While most of us wouldn't want our chapters read, her desire to share her healing overrides those feelings of being an "open book." Reading these stories reveals how far-reaching trauma can go. And how we see ourselves through the lenses of our parents. She reveals how it can affect all of our life choices.

In *The Rescue of an Orphan*, you'll learn how our skewed adult choices can seem normal, until we learn they're not. You'll see how hard it is to re-frame who we think we are, and change how we respond to life's struggles. Yet, that is not the end of the story—for out of each of those skewed choices, and the resulting pain, we see a glimpse of hope. And it is that hope that allows us to continue to heal, to believe change is possible, and to realize our story doesn't end with this "chapter." Woven throughout this book, one is drawn into understanding where true freedom comes from and discovering that it is only through our faith in God, who is the ultimate Rescuer.

How do I know this? Because I was given the privilege to walk beside her as she processed the trauma, to witness the incredible pain as she sought healing, and to see the beauty of a woman who walks with her head held high because she knows God is using her story as an instrument in reaching others with hope . . . for their rescue!

Lynette Wright, *Servant Leader*

You can't read Dean's *The Making of an Orphan* without immediately reading *The Rescue of an Orphan*. Her first book was the story of the author's younger years and foreshadows how the things that she experienced would affect her for decades. *The Rescue of an Orphan* continues her story into adulthood and to the day when she is rescued by God. It is a beautiful testimony of how our God can work despite the worst circumstances or experiences. I feel so privileged to know the author personally and to witness how deeply she cares about hurting people. By sharing her story with such vulnerability and passion, the author points to anyone who is hurting, to the One who is waiting to rescue them.

Felicia Warfel, *Seaford, DE*

Table of Contents

Foreword

Rescued…isn't that what we all want? To be Rescued. Leslie Dean laid the foundation in *The Making of an Orphan* by exposing how generational trauma impacts mind, body, and spirit. With her sequel, *The Rescue of an Orphan*, she shares her rescue journey in a transparent, vulnerable, relatable manner. She laid bare those places that she held so deep inside of her to give the reader hope in their darkness . . . and so they may realize that healing is possible. She highlights the importance of "doing the work" and gives reflective insight through her counseling perspective.

As a professional counselor, I find clients who, like Leslie, are unaware of veiling their experiences and hurts. They struggle through life—making the same bad decisions over and over—but wonder why things never seem to change. They cast blame on themselves and continue on the road to emotional, mental, physical, and spiritual destruction. It can be challenging for people to grasp what "doing the work" looks like. Leslie shares her story while authenticating the process.

This book will help those reading it to visualize therapeutic approaches, such as sitting with our younger selves. It will offer encouragement to my clients, and anyone else who picks it up . . . to trust the Father, and the process, of being rescued.

The Rescue of an Orphan is all about unrelenting love. And isn't that what we all want?

Patricia Boyce, PsyD, LPCMH, NCC

Acknowledgements

This is to all of those who sacrificed hours of their busy lives to help me review this book. You have been unrelenting in pressing on to reach the goal—through so many bumps in the roads of your lives . . . and mine. So many times, I wondered if I should keep going, and your encouragement saw me through. I doubt I will ever produce another book that was tougher to write than this one. Or one that was more transparent. I will forever keep your sacrifice in my heart to treasure. I love you all and appreciate you more than I am able to express in words.

Lynette Wright—It's been 33 years since I first walked into the Johnson Street Church of the Nazarene. Little did I know how much my life would change or how my new Sunday School teacher would play such a huge role in that change. These years have not always been easy on you. You have put up with a lot. Listened a lot. Given a lot. Supported a lot. And loved a lot. My gratitude is immeasurable. Someday we will be celebrating together in His presence. And I will thank Him every day for putting you in my life. Because . . . I made it there.

Colleen Morris— How can I thank you enough for all the late nights? All the formatting suggestions. All the edits. *All the things!* (LOL! a personal joke!) Your prayers and support have been priceless. You listened to a lot of raw stories, and talked me through a lot of times when I wanted to quit. You helped me immensely with my last two books, and your faith in me has never dwindled. You are my treasure.

Patsy Boyce—As always, you have been a cheerleader for me. Continuously pushing through to help me as a peer reviewer, even when your own life was so busy. Thank you for your vigilance.

Jeanette Hazel—It was our trip to Dallas that began this journey. I had a dream, and that trip found it fulfilled as I found a publisher and a new goal. You made that trip happen for me, and I am eternally grateful. And as always, thank you for your peer review guidance.

Dawn Robyn—What would I do without my visits to White Sulphur Springs during my writer's blocks? And your ever-present warm encouragements to keep going? You are an angel, and I can't thank you enough for providing the most peaceful place on the planet to complete my books.

Mona Hotchkin—Well, from one author to another, thank you for your encouragement and your love as we shared our many author's woes with each other. I always knew you understood as frustration took over when the words would not come. We walked through it together.

Wallace Rumbarger—Continued thanks for the ability to write my books because of your generosity. Many, many thanks.

Introduction

I am writing this book as a sequel to *The Making of an Orphan.* It was necessary to reveal the outcomes, or more appropriately, the consequences of what I experienced in childhood. How they played out for me as a person going out into the world, completely unprepared for life. Emotionally, I was stuck. In a lot of child-like thinking. And carrying a trunk full of unhealthy habits on my back.

I also want to address some of the questions that may have been raised in that book. I explained how the damage done to families is often generational because of what we learn from our mothers and fathers, or our caregivers. They teach us about parenting. And what they teach us we then pass on to our children. And most often, what they taught us was learned from their parents, and so on and so on. This is how intergenerational trauma, also known as transgenerational trauma, or generational curses, is passed down. If your parents were good parents, chances are you are a good parent as well. And you might have good grandparents, too. But if Mom and Dad were unhealthy, you may have grown up missing out on a lot of the ground rules for good parenting. And the worst part is, you probably don't realize it.

So, in *The Making of an Orphan,* I shared about my life growing up as Karin, in a very unhealthy family. A mother who was depressed most of the time and who punished with silent treatments or rages, and a dad who was either never home because of work, or when he was home, there was much control, gaslighting and unfaithfulness in his marriage. I did a lot of research to learn what caused these symptoms and shared how the generational trauma from their parents had been passed down. And passed down from their parents as well. It's insidious, but powerful, until someone realizes "This isn't right!" and tries to change things. Rocks the boat. Makes waves. And that isn't often received well . . . at all. Because "normal" is what's always been. No matter how sick it is. It's comfortable. And healing means change, and that's abnormal. It upsets homeostasis. It's *un*comfortable. So, anyone who tries to make it better, is targeted as "the bad guy." And that was me.

But before I learned all that, the way I was raised had consequences. Big consequences. For me. I learned if I couldn't get what I needed at home, I would find another way to get it. And if I couldn't find a way, I would make one. By numbing my pain. And with that came even more consequences, like addictions and unhealthy relationships. And that is the beginning of codependence. I learned that one like a champ. I could easily claim the queen's crown for codependency back in the day. I knew it well. We were best buds.

And there were other ways I acted out my pain. Some to get attention, some to hide from myself, some to please everyone else, and all to fill a giant hole in my soul. I was oblivious to any possible solution to fill that hole. None, I was aware of, or had ever been taught. And worse, I didn't even know I needed it. I had little knowledge of anything about life, or love, or what any of it was about. But Someone did. He knew exactly what I needed, and He was on the hunt for me. But I had to walk through a lot of hurt and pain before I chose to hear His voice. Before I chose to listen. Before I believed I could trust Him. I was used to doing things *my* way, for myself, because I had no one else to do them for me.

So, this book is about how a child can become an adult . . . having never really grown up emotionally. All of the traumas she experienced as a little girl are still inside. And they are acted out each time she is triggered by something. It's about all the ways she tries to numb the agony of those triggers. How long can she stuff it all before her own brain says, *I've had enough*, and she shuts down to living? How long can she cover up, hide, run, dissociate, or drink away her deepest longings for love and belongingness? How long can she survive with this much pain?

In the depths of all that hurt and complete helplessness, a Knight shows up . . .

and *The Rescue* is on.

Part One

And the Consequences Begin . . .

I've seen love come and
I've seen love walk away
So many questions
Will anybody stay?

It's been a hard year
So many nights in tears
All of the darkness
Trying to fight my fears
Alone, so long alone . . .

"Thank God I Do" by Lauren Daigle

1

Wise Words . . . Deaf Ears

I ended *The Making of an Orphan* by sharing about my relationship with Shang. I was still living in Rockville with my parents. It was a destructive and abusive time for me. And I was about to pay the penalties for never having learned the life lessons I so desperately needed. Though Shang was not Muslim, he still had expectations from his Iranian culture of how a woman should act and behave. I was way too American. And I had lied to him about my virginity because I didn't want him to think less of me. There was one before him whom I believed I loved, and who I thought loved me. Unfortunately, he had been the first in a long line of broken promises. Shang was the second. However, the guilt of lying to him caused my confession, and opened the door to the abuse and infidelity that followed. And I put up with it. I stayed. Because I thought I deserved it. And because the message from my mom was that if he hurt me, I must have done something to cause it. And from my dad, "He's a nice man. Things will get better." Nothing got better.

When he and his friends decided to go to school on the Eastern Shore of Maryland, I was excited to join him. He lived with two other students, and three more of his friends lived in the townhouse next door. They were all in the United States on student visas from Iran. I joined him soon after he moved in. Not a single argument from my parents. In fact, my dad made the 3-hour drive with a U-Haul to move my things for me. It was close to Crisfield, so I might get to see Aunt Ruby more often. My whole life, she had been my safe landing, and it was encouraging to know she would be close by.

I decided I would also take classes down here. I wanted to be a doctor, an OB/GYN, and signed up for four Gen/Ed classes working toward that goal.

3

The first few months of living with him were not too bad. But I should have known that wouldn't last.

First, he became jealous of the friends I hung around with in the neighborhood. The only people he wanted me to associate with were his friends, who were all guys. So, I tried hanging out with some of their girlfriends, and that was ok for a while. Though I had restrictions placed on me, he was allowed to do whatever he wanted without any discussion from me. If I did say anything about where he was going, I was told to shut up and he especially liked to do this in front of his friends. I knew two of the guys were cheating on their girlfriends, so I didn't trust he was any different. It sure wouldn't be the first time. I got a black eye when I mentioned to Shang that I knew they were cheating. It was "none of my business."

Things went downhill fast after that. He picked on everything I did. One of the guys living with us, the nicer one, Ali, moved out because he said he was tired of the way Shang treated me. He asked me why I put up with it, and I answered, "I love him." To which he replied, "That isn't love." Ali's defense of me only made things worse. They had argued when Ali left because it was going to cause a financial crunch for Shang and the other roommate. Somehow his leaving got dumped on my shoulders, and fault-finding became a daily exercise.

I went to visit Aunt Ruby, and her advice was to stick it out till the end of the semester and then break up with him. I didn't know how I could wait that long, and I didn't know how I could break up. It was a confliction I didn't understand. *The terms "trauma bond" or "codependency" were not in my vocabulary in those days, but I sure wish they had been.*

About 3 weeks before the end of the semester, Shang was picking on me about what I was making for dinner. I had learned to make many of the khordesh, or stew, he liked. This was a rich combination of meat and vegetables, and very delicious. Most of his friends told me mine tasted just like what they made at home, so all his recent complaining made little sense to me.

I had listened to it to almost every night for the last week, and I finally had had enough. I told him I was doing the best I could, and I was tired of his complaining. His reaction was instantaneous, and I found myself on the floor. I darted under the kitchen table next to the sliding glass door. He grabbed for me but couldn't reach me, so he removed his shoe and began to hit me wherever it landed. This was a familiar scene. I had been down this road with the shoe thing before, and I wasn't going there again. My brain was scrambling for the best escape route. I waited for a break, and clambered to the slider, grateful it was open. I slammed the door shut but knew I had little time.

Everyone I knew in the neighborhood was working, and I had only seconds to formulate a plan. I thought if he followed me to the front door, I could get in, lock it, and lock the slider before he could get back there again. Then I could call the police. I waited just long enough for him to see I was heading to the front door, and dashed in. It was almost too late. He was right there. If I could shut the door with my left hand, I could lock it with my right. The door's upper half was a 4-paned window, and as I went to slam the door, my left hand missed the wood and went through the glass. It exploded in his face. Simultaneously, I felt a paralyzing electrical shock run up my left arm. I looked down and saw a large sliver of glass sticking out of my wrist. I couldn't move my fingers or feel most of my hand. Time seemed to come to a standstill.

Shang was wiping glass from his face and his rage had seemingly dissipated when he saw my wrist. I had no medical training at this point other than what I learned as a CNA, so I pulled the glass out without thinking of the consequences. Blood immediately began pulsing from my wrist and I screamed at Shang to get a towel. I knew enough that this was an arterial bleed, and I needed to put pressure on it. The wound was gaping open to the bone. I was paralyzed with fear. He called an ambulance right away, and then my parents. My mom was hysterical, and called my dad who then called me. I told him what happened, leaving out the part about the beating. He told me he would call Bethesda Naval Hospital and then call me right back.

The ambulance arrived and the paramedics were able to stop the bleeding, placed a pressure dressing on the wound and began to get me ready to go to the hospital. Then Dad called. He had been told by the orthopedic surgeon I needed to get there as quickly as possible, so he was having them send a helicopter to the hospital in Salisbury. This was one time I appreciated my father's position. Being an admiral has its rewards. When I arrived at the local hospital, a surgeon was waiting and did some tests on my hand and confirmed, I needed surgery immediately if I wanted to save the use of the hand. He explained all the tendons had been severed, and the medial nerve. This was why I couldn't move it or feel it. He finished suturing the cut within minutes of the helicopter arriving. It was a quick trip to Bethesda.

A full team of doctors was waiting when I arrived and within minutes I was prepped for surgery. It was 7 pm when they put me under, and when I woke it was daylight. My arm was aching. It was wrapped in a huge dressing, hand to shoulder, resembling a cast, elevated on a pillow. The nurse was adjusting my IV, and welcomed me back. I asked how long the surgery took and she told me it had been 7 hours. The doctor operated on me throughout the night. "You're a lucky girl! The doc who performed your surgery just retuned form Vietnam. He served in a MASH unit in the field and is well rehearsed at putting bodies back together. He had to dig deep to find that nerve, but he was successful and anastomosed (put back together) the nerve. You might get some feeling back in that hand! And with some OT, you will be able to move it again."

The nurse was smiling and seemed to believe she was giving me good news. But all I heard was *I might* get feeling back in my hand. I was still so full of anesthesia, not too much was terribly clear, but that was crystal. She gave me a shot for the increasing pain, and it put me out of my thought processes for a few more hours. And that was a welcome relief.

I woke up with the doctor looking at my arm dressing. He was a pleasant looking man and smiling broadly. "You had a nasty cut there, girl! How did you do that? I gave him the "safe" story—leaving out the fight. "So, you just go slamming doors for no good reason?" I had the distinct impression he wasn't buying my story. "Was anyone on the other side of that door?" Nope. He wasn't buying it.

"I got into an argument with my boyfriend, and things got out of control. I was trying to lock him out. I missed the wood, and my hand went through the glass." I wasn't sure what to expect from him, and fearful I was getting Shang in trouble.

"If you have a boyfriend who chases you in anger, and who you feel you have to lock out of your home to feel safe . . . well, then, you need a new boyfriend. That is abuse and he should be in jail. Because of him, you may never be able to use your hand appropriately again. Do your parents know he treats you like this?"

I had never heard anyone speak to me about abuse, and never about Shang being abusive. I just took it as what I deserved—after all, wasn't that the message? And this thing about my hand was coming up again. "My parents know we have arguments. I probably do things to instigate the fights. But what do you mean about my hand? I had plans to be a doctor, an OB/GYN. I need full use of both my hands. What do you mean about not using it appropriately?"

He looked straight into my eyes and then at the floor. When his eyes met mine again, there was only sadness. "There is nothing you could do—in any shape or form—to this man that would warrant what happened to you. There is nothing you could do to deserve what you got. I am not worried about the tendons. They will heal in time, but you have severed the medial nerve. The nerve will grow back at about a millimeter a day. And even when it grows back, there is no guarantee you will have full sensory return. My best advice is to talk to your advisor in school. But I wouldn't put a lot of hope into that area of specialty. I am truly sorry."

His eyes told the story. Actually, both stories. My future as a doctor, and my ignorance in being in an abusive relationship. It almost felt like a new language in regard to Shang. My whole life, I had heard my parents blame each other for their feelings and I was consistently told how I "make" them angry. So, it made sense when I was told I set off Shang.

Let's take a quick break here. To the reader, let me say this with crystal clarity. You have no control over anyone else's feelings. You can't make anyone angry, sad, frustrated, happy, bored, etc. People are responsible for their own feelings. They have control of their feelings, and if they get angry, it is their choice to have that feeling. Often children hear from a young age, "You make me so angry," or "You make me so frustrated." This trains the child to believe they have the ability to control another's feelings. Welcome to the land of codependency where you feel you are either the cause of everyone's problems or the fixer of them. Trust me. You don't want to go there. Enough said.

After the doctor left, I had a lot to think about. After a few days, I went home. No one talked about what happened or how it happened. Dad went to Shang's and packed up my stuff and brought it home. Mom took good care of me, more nurturing than I had ever seen her. *Maybe relating to her own past?* I spent 3 weeks in the bulky dressing, and then it was replaced with just a local dressing, but I was fitted in a long plastic splint that kept my wrist in full flexion. The doctor told me it was mandatory that I didn't remove the splint, for any reason. The tendons and nerve had to remain in a stable environment until they completely healed. This was going to be a pretty crummy summer.

In August, I started Occupational Therapy (OT). The commander who worked with me was a beast. She didn't care about how much pain you were in; you needed to do the exercises. After several weeks, when she removed the splint, I was literally unable to move my wrist. It was "frozen" in place due to lack of movement. She explained to get the range of motion back, I needed to stretch the tendons by massaging them. Extending my wrist caused the tendons to look like arcs under my skin. It was kind of creepy, and painful, to massage them with cocoa butter and stretch them back out. The commander shared that damage to the medial nerve causes the thumb, index finger, middle finger and half the ring finger to lose sensation. And it prevents the thumb from being able to cross the palm to the pinky. "You will be able to move your thumb like that again, but you can't be lazy. Do the work every day and I will get you full range of motion in your wrist and your hand."

I didn't like her, but I believed her. For the next two months she pushed, I cried, and she pushed harder. One time she even made a "crybaby face" as if she was mocking me—and I hated her. And she used that hatred to push me harder. To "show" her I could do it. And it worked. In the end, I had no feeling in those parts of my hand (that would take years to return) but I had full range of motion in my wrist and my arm. On my last visit, I actually hugged her. And she told me she was proud of me, then added, "Leslie, your doctor told me what happened and how it happened. You are a beautiful, smart girl, and staying that way does not include that jerk you are with. Please think long and hard about what good you will miss if you stay with him. And what he might do to you next time. He is dangerous."

How I wish I had listened.

2

Closing a Chapter

Through all this, I was still in touch with Shang, but I was also doing things with my friends to keep busy. Most of them wanted me to get away from him for good, and would invite me to parties and other fun stuff. When I found out he was going back to Iran to visit family, a trip he took every year, I felt much more relaxed about doing things with them. He had always controlled who I hung with, and it had almost become a habit to feel guilty when I did what I wanted to do.

My friend Mary had started dating a really nice guy, Al, and she invited me to a party at his friend's house. I was excited because it was the first fun thing I had done since the accident. It was also fall, my favorite time of year. Though I couldn't feel my hand, I was able to use it pretty normally and wasn't as guarded about being around other people. I went with Mary to the party, and she introduced me to Al and Greg, who were hosting. It was Greg's parents' house, and in a very wealthy area. He had gone all out catering for it and it was quite impressive.

There seemed to be an immediate connection between Greg and me. He was a very nice guy, and treated me like I was a special guest. As nice as that felt, it also felt awkward after all the years with Shang. I thought maybe if I had a couple drinks, I might feel more relaxed. Greg made all of us cocktails and the party began. Though there was a lot of delicious food there, I didn't eat much at all. I was still hung up about people seeing me eat, and my dad's words of "men hate fat women" always played like a tape in my head. But I had no problem putting away the alcohol.

I have only a few memories of that night, and none of them were great. I recall feeling very sick and going outside to get fresh air. But the alcohol was putting everything in my gut in reverse, and after getting sick, I laid down in the grass. And that's about all I remember. Great first impression.

I woke up the next morning not knowing where I was. It was a strange room in a strange house. I was wearing a man's shirt over my bra and undies. What happened last night? I sat up in bed and looked out the window, and realized I was at Greg's house. Embarrassment and deep shame smacked me in the face. What had I done? He was a really nice guy, and I had completely blown it. I didn't even know if his parents were home. It was an unbelievable predicament. As all those thoughts shot through my foggy brain, there was a gentle knock on my door.

"Leslie, are you awake yet? I have some breakfast for you."

Oh, my gosh, I didn't know what to do. I didn't see my clothes anywhere, and so I pulled the covers up, covering me as much as I could. "Sure, I am awake. Come in."

Greg came in carrying a big tray and a bigger smile. "Good morning! How are you feeling? I made you some eggs and toast. I hope you're hungry!" The tray had a plate of eggs, bacon, toast, orange juice and tea . . . and a flower. Silverware wrapped in a napkin, and all the extras–butter, jelly and even honey. I was speechless.

"I brought you tea because last night when I offered you coffee, you said you didn't like it. How are you this morning? I think you drank a little too much last night on an empty stomach. After I found you asleep in the yard, Al and I were able to help you into the house and that's when I tried to give you some coffee. We were trying to wake you up so Mary could drive you home, but you were not in any shape to walk. After I realized you had gotten sick, and your clothes needed to be washed, I told them you could stay here."

I was so humiliated. There were not even any words. The more info he gave me the deeper the shame. "But what about your parents?"

"Oh, they are on the West coast visiting family. I couldn't go because of school. I washed your clothes, and left them in the bathroom for you. You are welcome to take a shower if you'd like." His smile was disarming. This all felt surreal . . . and uncomfortable. Then a thought occurred to me, a very embarrassing thought. "Greg, who took my clothes off and dressed me in this shirt? I don't remember that at all."

He immediately blushed. "Mary did, and I promise, I didn't look. You were able to help her a little bit. I just wanted to make you comfortable so you could sleep it off. I hope you're not angry."

Angry? I wasn't sure I had ever met a nicer guy. And I didn't question his word at all. I totally believed he had maintained as much of my privacy as possible. If he was any other kind of person, he could have taken complete advantage of me last night. No, he was who he said he was. In addition, I knew Mary would never leave me with someone unsafe. I was in complete wonder at a man like this. He had a chiseled, handsome face and strong build. And he was tall. Dressed more collegiately than I was used to—nice slacks and sweater, short haircut. But his care for someone he barely knew was a mystery. I could hardly take it all in.

"I am going to run down and get some coffee for me, so I can join you. I already went out for a run, and ate my breakfast, but would like to sit with you if its ok?" Mmmm. That smile.

"Sure, that would be great." We talked for more than an hour. It was Saturday morning, and he asked if I had any plans for the day. Of course, I didn't, so he said he would call Al and see if we could go out to his farm. Somewhere in our conversations the night before I shared my love for horses, and apparently Al's parents owned a horse farm. Al was all in, and said he would pick up Mary, and we could hang out at his house for the day. I grabbed a quick shower, and we were off. And what a wonderful day it was! He had a beautiful home in the country, on lots of acres. It was a glorious day.

Greg drove me home, and asked if he could take me out the following week. I could hardly believe how lucky I was! And we began to date pretty regularly. He was in school full-time, so we only got together on the weekends, but every weekend was special. I met his parents, who were very sweet, and we doubled a lot with Al and Mary.

After about 5 weeks of seeing each other, Greg told me he was taking me to a very special place for dinner. I thought everywhere he took me was special, but he said I needed to dress especially nicely for this date. I was intrigued! He picked me up and we drove to downtown DC. The restaurant had valet parking! It was incredible! I looked at the menu, but it was all in French and there were no prices. I had been taught well by Dad to always order the least expensive thing on a date, and I had been faithful to do that on all of my dates. So, I was in a bit of a quandary. Greg immediately saw my struggle, and ordered everything for us, after checking that I liked steak.

First, we had Asti Spumante, a delicious light and sparkly wine, similar to champagne, with a shrimp cocktail. Then the waiter brought in a large cart of food, and a grill. I had never experienced table side preparation of food before, especially Chateaubriand! He prepared a beautiful filet mignon, with sauteed veggies and tiny garlic potatoes. He served us the entree with freshly made croissants and whipped butter. Dad had taken us to a lot of nice places, but he would never spend money on a restaurant like this. It was incredible. Then to my surprise, he ordered dessert—Bananas Foster. Again, freshly made at the tableside. It was crazy good!

On the drive home, I thanked Greg for an amazing evening. We talked for a long time in front of my house, and he finally shared how much he cared for me. I felt a stab of guilt because I knew Shang was coming back the following week, and I didn't know how any of this would end up. I had been dating Greg for several weeks, but he had never even tried to kiss me. If he liked me as much as he said, why would that be? Don't you kiss people you say you care for?

I also still felt very uncomfortable with the kindness and care he exhibited. Not while we were together, but afterward, when I was alone. It was a different message than the one I was used to. A message of care and respect. Requiring nothing in return. It was so strange to me. With him not seeming to want more than spending time together, it all felt odd—extraneous. It certainly wasn't how it had been with others. All these thoughts were circulating in my head, when Greg put his arm around me, and asked if he could kiss me. And it was a wonderful kiss. He hugged me and told me he would call me about next weekend. Walking me to the door, he held my hand, and I didn't feel my feet touch the ground once. He kissed my forehead and said goodnight. I floated into the house.

How I wish I had hung onto those amazing feelings.

The next week, Shang came back from Iran. He was actually jovial when he called me and said he brought me lots of gifts. I didn't realize he had moved from the Eastern Shore back to the Washington area. He had taken time off from school to work to earn money for his last semester, and made the move just before his trip. The first week he was home, I was able to make excuses not to see him. When I saw Greg that weekend, I was actually scared the whole time that somehow Shang would find out. Greg picked up on how anxious I was, and asked what was wrong, but I lied and said I was fine. How is it that I felt so controlled—no, *owned*—by Shang? Like I had no right to do anything I wanted to do without his permission? But it was ingrained in me, and I didn't really enjoy my evening with Greg. So, when he tried to kiss me goodnight, I pulled away. This left us both confused.

The following day, Shang just showed up at my house. My parents treated him like nothing had ever happened. It was the first time they had seen him since the accident. I had never told them the whole truth about what happened, and had assumed the doctor might have. But it appeared he was still the great guy they always thought he was. I had never even told them about Greg. My parents paid little attention to my comings and goings, and I was afraid if they met Greg, it might get back to Shang. I had learned well how to keep secrets.

Shang took me to his new place where he had displayed all the things he had bought me on his bed. A beautiful necklace, a ring, a stained-glass lantern, a box of pistachio candy (very popular in Iran), a bag of pistachios, and a Persian embroidered lambskin jacket. It was pretty overwhelming. I was touched, and he seemed kinder since spending time with his family. I immediately felt guilty about Greg, and regretted starting that relationship.

Oh, here we go! This girl. If she only knew how stupid she was . . . and what she is about to give up.

It was almost Christmas, and Greg had asked if we could spend Christmas and New Year's Eve together. I had started to make excuses not to see him, and he was beginning to notice the difference in me. I would not commit to the holiday times, because I hoped I could spend them with Shang. So, I never said yay or nay, but just kept delaying. On the weekends, I continued to make up stories of needing to help out at home or needing to work.

Shang had taken his same job back at a popular restaurant in DC. This is the restaurant where he met the girl from England I shared about in *The Making of an Orphan*. I felt anxious every time he said he was going in. I just expected him to cheat on me again. He always told me not to worry about anything, but that was an impossibility. He promised to try to schedule himself off for the holidays, and so I finally told Greg I couldn't spend that time with him.

Mary called me that night. "Are you crazy, girl? What is going on with you? We have reservations for a New Year's party at this awesome restaurant in Virginia. Appetizers, dinner, open bar, live band, dancing, and a midnight champagne toast! It's going to be a blast! Greg has been feeling really hurt and feels you are pulling away. What's going on with you?"

I didn't know how to answer her. She was not a fan of Shang . . . at all. And she thought Greg was a great guy. "Mary, I have been so confused. Shang brought me all these awesome gifts from his home, and I know he loves me. He just loses his temper sometimes. He said he will try to get off to spend New Year's with me."

There was a long silence at the other end. Then a long sigh. "Les, you are a fool. Greg is so smitten with you, and he is a good man. What is wrong with you? Have you forgotten how your whole life has changed? All your plans to be a doctor? All your hopes and dreams—gone because of Shang. Have you forgotten all that?"

I wasn't in the mood to hear any of this. She didn't understand and she never would because she wanted me to stay with Greg so we could continue to double date and hang out. It was just her manipulating me for her own purposes. I didn't need her lectures. "Mary, I am sorry you don't understand how I feel about Shang. Yes, Greg is a great guy, but I have been with Shang for almost 4 years. And I love him." Mary hung up.

I want to take a break here and look into the twisted way I framed what Mary said. She was giving honest truth here. She was sharing what she saw and what she knew. She was not being manipulative. But I was unable to acknowledge that. So, the skewed thinking that accompanies trauma bonds started to show its ugly head. And it sounded like this: "No one understands him except me. No one can see what I see in this person. I must justify all his actions as worthy. I must deny any wrongdoing. I must protect him at all cost." Even if I am the one paying the price. This is the voice of the trauma bonded. This is the voice of codependence. This is the voice of a wounded little girl.

Well, a week later, Shang told me he couldn't get Christmas Eve off because they were having a private party. And he wasn't terribly sorry about it because he would be making "big bucks." He said New Year's was possible, but nothing confirmed yet. Then, on the morning of New Year's Eve, Shang cancelled on me. No apology. He just had to work. I cried most of the day.

That afternoon, I got a great idea. It had only been a few weeks since I had told Greg I couldn't go to the New Year's party. Maybe I could still go with him. He would probably be really happy to hear from me. So, I called him. "Hi, Greg. It's Leslie. I am so sorry I haven't been in touch lately, but things have been crazy. It turns out I am free tonight, and I would love to spend New Year's with you!"

I had not talked with Greg for a while, but I knew his voice pretty well. It had always been kind and gentle, but that wasn't the case today. He was still kind, but there was firmness and authority I had not heard before. Certainly nothing I expected. "Hi, Leslie. It's nice to hear from you. I am sorry you will be alone tonight. I have already asked another girl for the New Year's party, and I won't cancel on her. I hope you are able to find something fun to do. Take care." And he hung up.

It literally felt like my heart had hit the floor. Not just because I wasn't going with him, but the difference in the way he sounded. He had never spoken to me like that, and I realized immediately how deeply I had hurt him. And worse, any chance of a future with him was over. I wallowed in that for a little while, but then soothed myself with the thought that I still had Shang.

Some thoughts here. I was well acquainted with feeling rejected so this was familiar to me. Trying to wrangle my way back into the New Year's party with Greg, so I wouldn't be alone, is what a child would do. If I can't have the toy I want, I will get a different toy. This was my first experience with a healthy man. It was so wonderful . . . and so confusing. I had been trained that sex and love were the same, so being treated with respect, being treated as I deserved to be— being treated as a lady—was all foreign to me. I felt his lack of wanting to be sexual with me was rejecting me. And that's when I started to question the relationship. I heard a voice in my head saying, "He doesn't love you. He doesn't want you. He is just passing time with you till someone else comes along." And that voice became dominant in my brain. So, by the time Shang returned, the bait had been laid. And I took it. And lost something amazing.

It had felt that Shang had some degree of sorrow for the accident, and he apparently felt the gifts he gave me covered his part in it. I was now free all the time, and he would take me to his new place, so we could hang out with his new roommates. I was, again, limited in who I could spend time with. It went well through most of January, probably because we both had birthdays this month, but soon things turned sour. His roommates were "too friendly" to me. One in particular, Mahmood, was extremely caring. I knew him before Shang had moved to the Eastern Shore. He was one of the guys we hung out with in DC. And now he was very attentive. Brought me tea, food, anything I needed. Shang would speak to him in Farsi, and I knew most of what was being said. I had picked up quite a few words, and he was basically telling him I can do things for myself. Mahmood ignored him. Once when Shang went to the store, Mahmood told me I needed to leave him, that he didn't deserve me. He also shocked me by telling me he was in love with me. And that made things really awkward going forward.

As the weeks passed, Shang's old ways started showing up again. I thought about breaking up with him and just couldn't handle the thought of being alone. We had been together for 4 years. It felt very scary for me to be alone. So, I hung on. One evening we watched TV, and Mahmood made dinner. He brought me some tea which initiated a tirade from Shang. Then he brought me dinner, and Shang went off. Hassan, the other roommate, was home and told him to calm down, but he kept yelling at Mahmood. Then both Hassan and Mahmood tried to calm him down, but in his rage, he shoved my plate onto the floor. I jumped up and went into the closest bedroom, which was Mahmood's room, fearful it would get physical. I listened to them argue for a while and then heard the front door slam shut.

Mahmood came to the room. "He's gone. Are you okay?"

I was crying and relieved Shang had left. "I don't know what to do anymore, Mahmood. He scares me when he is like this." He had put his arm around me, and it felt safe . . . until he kissed me. The initial fear of being caught melted into the gentleness of this kiss. Not like Shang's at all. Yes, more like Greg's had been.

I don't know how long we were kissing, but Hassan finally knocked on the door and the magic of that moment ended. The fear of being caught was now overwhelming. Mahmood got up and answered the door and said everything was fine, but the rest was said in Farsi, and Hassan was angry. I got my coat and left. Mahmood tried to follow me, but Hassan stopped him.

And that is how my chapter with Shang ended. Hassan apparently told Shang what had happened between Mahmood and I. Shang confronted him. He admitted his feelings for me, and he was made to move out. Shang called me, and we met near my house. He asked me if it was all true and I admitted it was. He told me about Mahmood's confession and then casually volunteered he had promised to kill Mahmood if he ever came near me again. If he couldn't have me, no one else would either. And that was the last time I saw him.

3

A New Lesson

When you are a codependent, you can't stay alone for very long. Of course, I didn't know I was a codependent. That was a term I wouldn't be familiar with for another 14 years. But my symptoms were in full swing. I had just learned my parents were moving back to Seattle, and I needed to find a place to live. Ivy, my out-of-control neighbor you met in *The Making of an Orphan*, offered to let me stay with her, but I wasn't keen on that. I had also learned from my advisor at school that becoming an OB/GYN was out of the question since my left hand did not have full sensory return. And it never would. This was another life slam I could add to the tennis- pro hopes and horse ownership disappointments I had as a child. So, I was a prime target to escape into a new relationship.

Since my breakup with Shang and my disaster with Greg, my friends and I had been hitting all the local hang outs on the weekends. My friend Heather had heard about a party at a friend's house, so we decided to check it out. The apartment was small, and it was packed out. There was a keg on the balcony and plenty of liquor in the kitchen. The room was foggy with smoke—all kinds. Heather and I had already had some wine before we got there, so we were relaxed and ready to party. I quickly noticed the tallest guy in the room, and he was pretty nice looking as well. One thing that always bugged me about Shang was being an inch taller than he was, so I could never wear heels. This time I was going to be a little pickier.

I found a spot near him, and acted casual, till he eventually noticed me. Apparently this was his apartment, and he asked if I needed a drink. We talked very comfortably, and it was obvious there was a connection. He introduced himself as Nick, and throughout the evening, he stayed pretty close to me. I was definitely attracted. As people started filtering out, he asked how long I could stay, and since it seemed Heather had made a friend also, I was cool to hang longer. Eventually, only the four of us were left and Nick sat on the couch next to me. We talked for a while, but pretty soon we were making out. He was a gentleman in every other way, and asked me if he could see me again. We exchanged phone numbers, and Heather and her friend did the same. After we left, I told her what a great guy he was, and couldn't wait to see him again. *Oh, my. And so . . . it begins.*

Nick called the next day, and I went to his apartment, and we watched a football game. His roommate came home, and brought another 12-pack of beer. Nick had almost gone through the one he had bought earlier. I wasn't much of a beer drinker, so I was drinking vodka tonics. I didn't pay much attention to the beer thing, until I noticed his roommate drank only 3 of the beers he had brought home, and Nick drank the rest. But what blew my mind is he didn't act drunk. After the game, his roommate went to his room, and Nick and I just talked. During our conversation, I shared with him my predicament with my parents moving, but not expecting what came next. He asked me if I wanted to move in with him. Without me responding, he went to his roommate's room and asked if it was ok with him. Within minutes, it was a done deal. I couldn't believe my luck! I was so enamored by his generosity we ended up sleeping together.

Ok. We are going to take a little break here, because even as I write this, I want to grab that girl and give her a solid shake to wake her up! It is so hard to be transparent and write about how completely ignorant I was about life and relationships. How completely unhealthy I was to jump into so many stupid situations with my eyes wide shut. Looking for love in all the wrong places.

But I also have to offer her some grace. Because how do you know right from wrong, good from evil, if no one has ever taught you? And no one had ever taught me anything. These are the consequences of what Karin experienced in The Making of an Orphan. *This younger version of Leslie you met in that book, was only taught she wasn't good enough. That she was a sexual object. These are the aftereffects of being neglected and abused with no attachment to a healthy parent. You accept anything or anybody who will give you any form of attention. No matter how it feels or how much it hurts.*

This is most often passed down generationally—the trans-generational trauma I wrote about in The Making of an Orphan. *Codependence is passed on like a baton in a relay race. Let me give you a quick definition of codependency. Simplistically, it's an addiction to relationships. More specifically, it's an addiction to relationships that are one-sided, emotionally destructive and/or abusive. Sound familiar? That's why I found the healthy and decent men boring.*

I found an awesome quote from the book, "The Perks of Being a Wallflower." The protagonist shares with his teacher that his sister is being hit by her boyfriend, and he doesn't understand why she allows it. His teacher's face forms a very somber look, and responds, "We accept the love we think we deserve." (Chbosky 25)

This could have been my mantra.

I told my parents I had found a place, but left out the part about it being with a guy. They were both happy about that since they were leaving within the month. They agreed to take my dog, Reeshie, with them to Seattle until I was able to find a place that accepted pets. Neither asked to see the place or meet my roommates, so it went pretty quickly. Nick borrowed a truck and moved my stuff for me. And life began as his live-in girlfriend. I was amazed at how many parties these guys had. Every weekend there was a keg party. I noticed over time how much beer Nick could put away and still be functioning pretty normally. I had little knowledge of addiction or alcoholism at this point, but I was getting my first lessons. On the job training.

One weekend Nick wanted to take me to meet his parents. He had a pretty awesome classic car that he took to their house to wash every week. They lived in the country in a home similar to those in Crisfield. His mom made us an early supper, so he and his dad could watch the football game. They seemed like nice people, though his dad was putting away as many beers as Nick. He kept asking his wife to bring him things to snack on, and she obediently did it—almost robotically. The more he drank, the more demanding he became. I was beginning to feel uncomfortable, and his mom seemed nervous. At one point she said she was going outside to work in the garden, and he told her she would "stay in the house, in case I need you." Her meek response confirmed my observation.

I looked at Nick, expecting a response—to maybe defend his mom—but he never even looked away from the TV. Like this was a regular thing. I sat quietly, not sure what to expect. The game ended and Nick said we could go down to the basement and play some Nintendo. I was relieved to go anywhere away from his dad. We had been playing a game for about an hour when I heard yelling from upstairs. Then I heard a banging. I asked Nick if everything was okay and he blew me off saying, "Oh, they are just arguing. No biggy." When I heard her start crying for him to stop, I stood to go see if she was ok, and Nick pulled me back down on the couch.

"This is none of your business, and its none of mine. Sit down and shut up." Then he went back to playing his game. Inside, I was terrified. My heart was pounding, and I wanted to run up there to help her. This was pretty fresh for me. So many times, I had hoped someone would come and help me when

Shang went off. I could hear her crying and decided to help her no matter what Nick said. I slid toward the side of the couch closest to the steps to make a dash for it before Nick could stop me. But he was quick. He grabbed me, throwing me back on the couch, and putting his forearm over my neck, pinned my head against the arm of the sofa. Then he punched me in the mouth. The pain was exquisite. Running my tongue over my teeth, I felt one had been chipped. I tasted salt, and knew my mouth was cut. He was pushing into my neck, and it was getting harder to breathe. His face was contorted. He looked nothing like himself.

"You will do what you're told! You get any ideas about thinking on your own, just forget them. You buck me and I will teach you a lesson you won't forget!" His breath stunk of beer. Lots of it. I began to believe he was going to kill me, but was paralyzed to fight back. In a few seconds, he released the pressure on my neck, and pulled me upright on the couch. I couldn't speak. I couldn't move. I thought I may pee my pants. Then he smiled.

"Okay, that's better. Just relax. I am going upstairs and see if everything is ok, and you stay here." He leaned over and kissed me on the forehead and went upstairs. I was in shock. Things with Shang had been bad, but this? I wanted to run but was unable to move. I wanted to see if his mom was ok. And I wanted to know how I got here again. This time I wouldn't be stupid like I was with Shang. I will leave as soon as he goes to work tomorrow.

He came back down and said we were leaving. My mouth felt swollen. He saw me checking it and kissed me. "It doesn't look bad." Wow! Just like that! As calm as a cucumber. I was so confused. Shang stayed mad after his explosions until later when he brought the gifts to apologize. But this? Like nothing had happened at all. This was so nuts.

We went upstairs, and his mom was nowhere around. His dad was still watching TV and waved as we went past. We drove home in silence and when we got to the apartment he told me to go in, and he would be right up. I assumed he was going to buy more beer, so I obeyed. Tomorrow I will get my chance to get out. Not sure how to get my stuff moved, but I would be out. I went straight to the bathroom to look at my face. Yep, it was swollen and one of my front teeth was slightly chipped. Thank goodness it wasn't terribly noticeable. I took a quick shower, got into my PJ's, and when I had come out of the bedroom, Nick was back. He had bought a dozen red roses, my favorite wine, Asti Spumante, and a beautiful bracelet that said, *I love you.* He had not said that to me yet.

He looked sheepish as he put the bracelet on my wrist and had tears in his eyes. "I am so sorry, Leslie! I don't know what got into me. It will never happen again, I promise. Please, please forgive me. I do love you, and I don't want to lose you." He hugged me so tenderly, kissing my forehead. And that was that. I was butter in his hands. I wouldn't move out because this meant he truly loved me. Forgive. Forget. No worries . . . until the next time.

And there were many more "next times." The "honeymoon" stuff was so addictive. It's the make-up session where the abuser lavishes words of love, gifts of forgiveness, and any other manipulative thing he can do to keep the victim with him. It always follows the explosive stage— often the physical violence. But the "honeymoons" are always so sweet. You tend to live for the honeymoon. You might even instigate a fight—just so you can "earn" the honeymoon. This is the course people take in the domestic violence cycle. And a couple of other things I want you to notice. Did you see the part where she felt she couldn't move? Like she was paralyzed? That's the adrenaline rush—and the response is fight, flight, or freeze. Whichever part of your brain that has taken over your crisis response, this is how your body responds in these situations. It's not within your control.

And the other thing I want you to notice was his response to her swollen lip. "It doesn't look bad." That's gaslighting. Downplaying or outright lying about a situation so the victim starts to question their own sanity. These are the games played in domestic violence. The honeymoon is the "love bomb" you wait for as you go through the rest of the cycle. It's how a trauma bond is formed. It's why both women and men stay in abusive relationships. They don't know—because they haven't been taught—there is a history in their lives that set them up for this. It's why they choose these types of relationships. And they will stay until there is a crisis moment that finally wakes them up. And then they leave that relationship, but drift into another one just like it. It feels like a hopeless cycle. One they don't know how to break out of. This was me. And I stayed in this one for many more cycles. Until my crisis moment got me out. And this one was even worse than the crisis moment with Shang.

This one changed how I defined myself.

4

The Whispering Voice

Going to parties with Nick was a frequent thing. Going to a party at the home of a girl who unashamedly flirted with Nick was going to be a challenge. He assured me there was nothing between them; she acted that way with everyone. I didn't recall ever seeing her sit in anyone else's lap at the Ale House, or fluff anyone else's hair, or blow kisses to anyone else. These seemed to be specific to Nick, even when her boyfriend was with her.

We arrived fashionably late—not because I wanted to but because Nick had to buy a 6- pack and down the whole thing before we arrived. So, I knew the evening was going to be an adventure. The woman in question greeted us at the door with a quick "hello" to me but a full-on hug and lip kiss to Nick. Didn't care one bit that I was standing right there. She was clearly lit already, and whispered something to him. She took his jacket, hung it up and led him into the living room, leaving me at the door. The way she was acting was a clear message they had crossed a line of friendship—I just didn't know how or when.

The living room was packed, the mixed smell of cigarettes and pot smoke almost nauseating. I noted the "happy bowl" on the coffee table—a rainbow of pills and capsules. Those always scared me because no one knew what they might be taking—and I had seen enough examples of bad trips and bad side-effects to stay clear. I saw Nick getting a burger and she was doting on him offering him food samples from the picnic table. He seemed oblivious to my whereabouts and my heart began racing.

A tap on the shoulder brought me back from dark thoughts. It was my lab partner from a chemistry class I had taken here before I moved. Organic chemistry was one of my favorite subjects and we were good buddies. He engaged me for a while in catching up, sharing he had gone on to pre-med and asking if I had continued to pursue my dream of being an OB/GYN. I gave him the short version of what happened to my hand, but that I had begun pursuing nursing. He offered me a drink which I gladly took, guzzled it down, and asked for another. His facial expression made me chuckle, and I assured him I would be okay.

After yet another drink, he offered to go get us some dinner, and the air outside was refreshing. I had temporarily forgotten to keep track of Nick, and was enjoying the time spent with my friend. Someone announced there was a game of charades going on in the basement. I loved games, so we joined in on the fun. It wasn't until my friend said he had to go home to study that I realized I hadn't seen Nick in a while. I dismissed it, hugged him goodbye and decided to make another drink. In the kitchen, a couple girls were getting ice, and I overheard one say she had not seen our hostess for a while, asking the other if she had. Ahh, that familiar, sinking feeling was immediately present in my gut.

Her home was a large end unit townhouse, and I had only seen 3 of the rooms. I left the kitchen deciding to investigate the rest of the house and the whereabouts of Nick. Before I left the kitchen, I poured another few shots into my glass. I knew I was going to need it. The kitchen opened up into the living room, which was full of people. No Nick. I checked outside once again, asking a few people, but no one had seen him. I did another round in the basement and even checked the bedroom down there. Coming back up to the main floor, I realized I had finished my drink already, and was feeling the familiar buzz. My heart was racing, and my body was on full alert as I anticipated what I would see when I found them. I checked out the upper level. Both bedrooms were empty. Interestingly, I had not checked the master bedroom yet, maybe trying to postpone the inevitable. Back downstairs, I left the living room, and noticed another room on the left. It was an unusual place for it, but it was possibly a formal dining room. As I approached the doorway, the sounds I heard were unmistakable. Drowned out by the music till now, but clearly obvious.

I had a moment of pause. If I didn't look, I wouldn't know for sure. If I didn't look, I could pretend nothing happened. Dismissing my last attempt to stay in denial, I knew I had to know the truth, and quietly leaned around the doorway. On the opposite side of the room was the dining room table. Two people were on it. And so intensely pre-disposed, they didn't even notice me. No question it was Nick. The only light present was the little bit coming from the living area. The scattered clothes on the floor didn't escape me. My heart was pounding, breaths coming in measured gasps.

I found myself in the kitchen. The half empty bottle of vodka on the counter, I downed in a few swallows. Standing at the sink, grasping the counter to steady myself, the tears poured out of me. This couldn't be happening—not again. Another fiancé betrayal. *Yeah, you read that right. During one of our many "honeymoons" he had proposed and given me a ring. And I had said "yes."* Here is another man who had brutalized me, and I had put up with it so I could just be loved. The tears were hitting the sink with such regularity, I checked to see if the faucet was dripping. I was frozen. Physically. Mentally. Emotionally. I didn't even know how to get home. Thoughts were racing when I felt a strong arm hug me. Hoping it was Nick, I turned, but it wasn't. It was his friend Sven. I had met him at a few parties, and he had always been very friendly.

"What's wrong, Les? He grabbed a paper towel and began to wipe my face. I turned back to the sink and sought hard for the words, but finally just vomited out the pain in my reply.

"Nick is screwing someone on the dining room table. We were supposed to be engaged. I feel like my heart is breaking in pieces."

He turned me around and hugged me hard. Then he stepped back and reached for his pocket, pulling out a pill. "Take this and you will forget all about Nick and what he is doing. Trust me, it will make it all go away!"

I didn't need to be asked twice. It looked like a Quaalude, so I took it from his hand, popped it in my mouth, grabbed a half empty beer on the counter, and guzzled it down. He held me for a time, I have no idea how long, but it was the last thing I remembered.

When I woke up, I was on a bed, and there were five guys all around me. Sven was near my head, kissing me, and the others were all doing something different. It took me a moment to comprehend what was happening, but when I did, I began screaming for them to stop. At that moment I realized I was naked . . . and so were they.

Sven looked shocked. "You don't want this?"

I screamed in his face, "No, no, no! Please stop!"

He immediately stood up and told the others to stop. Two of them backed off, picking up their clothes off the floor. But his request wasn't received well by all. When Sven insisted, one of the guys threw a punch at him and a fight broke out with the remaining two. I had enough cognizance to realize this was my chance to get out. I didn't know where my clothes were, so I wrapped myself in the bedspread and ran toward the bathroom. My head was pounding, and my body felt like rubber. Like I was moving in slow motion. My jeans and shirt were at the foot of the bed, and I grabbed them as I ran past. I had to stop a few times and grab onto something. I was so dizzy. The fighting was escalating so I dressed as fast as I could.

As I maneuvered my way out, I stumbled over one of the guys on the floor. He was knocked out. It seemed Sven was the stronger of the three and had taken on both of them. Trying to run, I was scrubbing up against the hallway wall to keep my balance. I had no shoes, but I was not going back. The house was dark. How much time had passed? Had Nick just left me here? If I had been in the master bedroom, then where were they? My head was pounding too hard to go there. Crossing through the kitchen toward the front door, I picked up the bottle of Kahlua that was on the counter. I also grabbed a pack of cigarettes left there.

Outside, the air was cool, and off to my left the sky was brightening. Birds were singing their morning songs. It must be close to dawn. I walked to the side of the house where there were some bushes, and sat down behind them. I needed time to figure out what I was going to do. The chill that was refreshing when I first came out, soon became uncomfortable, but it was helping to clear my head. I didn't know if I was just badly hungover or if the pill Sven had given me was causing all the brain fog. I was grateful for the Kahlua. It took the edge off what my head was doing, and the chill. I don't know how long I sat there, but the liquor did its job, and I eventually fell asleep.

"Les, are you okay?" I heard the voice as part of my dream, but the persistence of it awakened me. It was Sven. I didn't know whether to hug him or slug him. He must have read what was in my mind because he slid down beside me and hugged me tightly, apologizing profusely for giving me the pill. I didn't think to ask him how things escalated from the kitchen to the bedroom. That part of my brain would wake up later. Soon he started apologizing for the rest of it. I asked no questions. I didn't want to know any details. The events of the evening were too overwhelming for me to face right now. Way too much had gone down.

"I left my shoes, and I don't know where I am or how to get home. Nick drove and obviously he left me here." My voice was muffled because he was holding me so tight. Momentarily, I began to feel safe in his arms. This should have been Nick holding me. Comforting me. Loving me. Instead, it was one of his friends.

After a while, he got up and went to try the door. "We can't get back in. The door is locked. But I can drive you home if you don't mind riding with me." He went into another litany of apologies for allowing any of it to happen, saying he had always liked me, and had actually hoped Nick and I would break up. That was more info than I was able to take in.

The sun had come up and for the first time, I noticed his face. He had definitely been in a fight; his left eye was swollen, and he had a pretty bad cut on his lip. He was Swedish and had very long, thick, blond hair, some of which carried the evidence of the blood from his lip. I had always thought he was a handsome guy, but all these hugs and apologies seemed to make him even more attractive. Confused and still so drugged and drunk, I knew I needed to take him up on the offer to drive me, but I wasn't about to go home and find her in my bed with Nick.

"Sven, I can't go home because I think Nick probably took her with him. I am not sure what to do."

He didn't hesitate. "I will take you to my place. I live alone. You can get a shower, get some sleep and then I can make you breakfast."

His smile was sweet, and his caring words and offers were as well. I bet he never hit any of his girlfriends! This formed an ugly memory of one of Nick's beatings in the basement of his house, after drinking all day. There were many times I felt certain he could kill me. I had heard his father do the same to his mother, so it was in the blood. This beating had been because I talked to a friend I knew from school at the Ale House one night. He said I was flirting, which was ridiculous because the guy was with his wife, but it was impossible to reason with him when he was drunk. Why was I thinking of this now? I couldn't go there. I made a conscious effort to push all that out of my mind. A skill I had mastered during my years with Shang. Forcing myself to return to the present, the idea of getting cleaned up and sleeping off all the remaining junk in my body felt like a really good idea.

I agreed and he left to get his car. He had a big, older car like my Dad's Bonneville. He opened the driver's door and had me get in first, then slipped in next to me. After starting the car, he put his arm around me and pulled my head to his shoulder. This felt almost too good.

His apartment was really nice, and well decorated. I had never asked Sven what kind of work he did, but it seemed he was doing okay. He immediately showed me where his bedroom was, and it felt good to lie down. My head was slowly improving. I felt like I could sleep for days.

I was drifting when Sven came into the room, two drinks in hand. "I thought a drink would take the edge off. I also have some weed. I just want you to relax."

I definitely didn't need anything else to drink, and my marijuana days were long gone. "No, thanks, Sven, but I appreciate the thought. I just want to sleep. I want to forget everything that happened. At least for a while." He downed his drink and asked if he could lie next to me and sleep also. I actually thought that it could be kind of nice and moved over in the bed. After he got in, I rolled to my side away from him and waited for the sweet seduction of sleep. But Sven had a different seduction in mind. He began rubbing my back and soon his objective was obvious.

"What are you doing, Sven? I thought we were going to sleep and recoup. My head is still in a fog." He leaned in and tried to kiss me, but I pulled away. I felt some weird allegiance to Nick all of a sudden and felt I shouldn't be doing this with one of his friends. "I can't do this, Sven. I can't do this with one of Nick's friends. Maybe I should get up and have you take me somewhere."

His face revealed his confusion. "Why would you feel any kind of loyalty to him? He not only screwed another girl at the party where he took you, he then left you there, and probably took her back to your apartment. You don't owe him anything!"

What? This coming from the guy who drugged me and led me into an orgy? My breath caught in my throat. Wait. What? Orgy? The word had almost been whispered in my ear. I participated in an orgy? Things were being reframed in my head at the speed of sound. Only whores did that. Sluts. The girls whom guys call "easy." And a few other names I don't want to even think about. I was suddenly in a dark place, and none of Sven's words were even audible. I felt dirty and disgusting. I could not believe I had stooped so low. I suddenly didn't even feel worthy of having sex with him. I had experienced a paradigm shift from someone who felt she had been a victim, to someone who participated in an act I felt was repulsive. I desperately wanted a drink, and after Sven sat up, I grabbed what he had made me and downed it.

Sven looked confused and hurt. He felt the change in me, and I didn't want to be around him anymore. I asked him to take me home. He argued about the possibility of Nick being there, but I didn't care. I was going to pack my stuff and get out anyway. He reluctantly agreed, but it wasn't until we got to the apartment that I realized I didn't have my keys. In fact, I didn't have my purse. I had left it in Nick's car before the party so I wouldn't forget it if I drank too much.

Now what? I didn't want to see anybody I knew, and I couldn't drive my car anywhere— no keys. I noticed Nick's car was not there either. So, I asked Sven to drive me to Ivy's. Good old reliable Ivy. I should tell Sven he probably has a really good chance with her. She liked young guys. He took me to her house and attempted to kiss me, but I wasn't having it. I thanked him and said goodbye, and that was the last time I ever saw Sven.

Ivy didn't ask any questions. I told her I just needed sleep, and probably a ride later on to pick up my car. I lay on the same familiar bed in her basement, staring at the same ceiling I had stared at all those years ago when I was first awakening to this highway of life I found myself on. I was definitely not the innocent and naïve girl I was back then. This highway had taken me to some painful places. Some terrifying places. Places no person should ever go.

At least that's how I felt before last night. But now I was this girl who did bad, bad things. So maybe I deserved all that pain, including the beatings and betrayals. As I lay there, it was almost as if these thoughts were being whispered in my ear. Like when I had heard "orgy." The *voice* wanted me to know what a pathetic person I was. A voice I was familiar with—like an old friend.

My parents often remarked on how someday I would get what I deserved. It has taken a while, but now, at 22 years old, I guess it is happening. Last night had added a lot more weight to the words of my *old friend*.

By the way, this was not a friend I chose, but one I had met at a young age, and one whom I could depend on to remind me of all my mistakes. A voice who stayed very close to me for the next several years and who I listened to far too often. A voice that knew every shame- filled thing I had ever done . . . and loved to remind me of each and every one. And especially seemed to enjoy watching me wallow in that shame.

A voice I would someday learn . . . was the enemy of my soul.

5

A Voice of Reason

I would like to say I did the right thing for myself after all that. But that just wasn't within my ability. Even after the cheating and the abuse, I still saw Nick. I did move out after the incident at the townhouse. And of course, the engagement was off. I called my dad and made up a story about losing the apartment. Dad called his best friend who quickly agreed to allow me to stay with him and his wife until something else became available. I had known this couple since I was in elementary school. She had been a teacher in my school in Aberdeen, and I had always had a secret crush on him from the day I met him. Our families vacationed together almost every summer. I had not decided if I was going to introduce them to Nick or not, but at least I had a safe place to sleep.

Even though Mom and Dad had moved, I continued going to the commissary to buy food and cigarettes since I still had my government ID. I had noticed a guy who worked there, a bagger, who was very attractive. The rugged type. We had exchanged niceties on a few occasions, and recently he had asked me out. His name was Doug, and he seemed nice. So, I gave him my phone number, but found myself making excuses whenever he called me. Then I ran into him at a club where Camelia and I had met to go dancing. I loved to dance, and if no one else asked us, we danced together. After a particularly long set, I was completely dehydrated and stopped to get some water on the way to our table. A guy approached me, and he looked familiar. It was dark and at first I couldn't recall how I knew him. Then I realized it was Doug. He looked even more awesome out of the uniform he wore at the commissary, and when he introduced himself, I was impressed. He complimented me on my dancing and joined me for the next song. We danced the rest of the night.

Camelia left early, and he and I talked quite a bit between dances. After many requests that night, I finally agreed to go out with him.

The following evening, Doug picked me up and took me to an amazing restaurant. Not quite like the place Greg took me, but the food was outstanding. We talked so easily—like we had known each other for a long time. He shared that his parents were both doctors, one worked at the Navy hospital, and one worked at the NIH. He said he was just bagging0 at the commissary while he went to school—also to be a doctor. Pretty impressive. We had a wonderful night and when he dropped me off he thanked me and made no effort to do anything except a kiss on the cheek. Hmmm.

Well, here we go again. It took me very little time to convince myself he definitely didn't like me—not like a girlfriend, anyway. What was wrong with me? My thoughts went back to Nick. Even with all that had happened, he did seem to want me. And like Dad had taught me, if I made sure the sex was good, then I would always have a boyfriend. So, in my perfunctory thinking, if there was no desire, there was no love. And that meant I probably wouldn't be seeing Doug again.

Oh, boy. So, I could begin the same lecture here I did before, but again I must offer grace because one can't be held responsible for what they don't know. In The Making of an Orphan, *I shared how my dad had given me two books, at age 15, on how to perform sexually, and promised me if I learned those things, I would never be without a boyfriend. What was the message? That sex was my purpose. What he did was objectify me. I was defined by how well I could perform, and it taught me that sex and love were synonymous. So, when someone didn't make a move on me in a sexual way, I immediately jumped to the conclusion, they didn't love me. It was so backwards, and because of that twisted thinking, I ended up leaving behind the "boring" guys (the gentlemen), the ones with which I might have had a promising future. Instead, I chose those who wanted sex, and who ended up having little else in their toolbelt to offer me, especially not a healthy or lasting relationship. The books, the message from my father, plus the rest of my childhood rejection and neglect, had set me up for making choices based on a negative self-perception. And it was going to take a miracle to change that thinking.*

The next time I ran into Doug at the commissary, I evaded his bagging line, and tried to avoid him altogether. But as my luck would have it, he saw me and waved. As I approached the door to leave, I stopped to say hi and he flashed that big smile. "Where have you been, girl? I have been trying to get up with you for over a week. Have you been sick?"

Ugh! Here we go. I didn't know how to maneuver this one. "I have just been busy. I have been babysitting for the people I live with (lie) and I didn't get your messages (lie). How have you been?"

"Missing you! Would you like to go dancing this weekend? I have both nights free. We could do dinner first?"

This was getting deep. How do I dodge this one? "Doug, I will have to give you a rain check. I just haven't been feeling the best. Maybe touch base next week?"

The disappointment on his face surprised me. And what he said next did even more. "Les, if you don't want to go out with me, just say so. I'm a big boy; I can handle it." I totally didn't expect that. "Take care of yourself, Les." Then he walked away. Just like that.

Let's look at that response. Here was a man who knew how to use his words and express them appropriately. But it was Greek to me. Definitely something I had never witnessed growing up. No manipulation. No games. No anger. Just putting it out there. Just like Greg had done. Unlike me who was playing the dodge ball game. I was dumbfounded—and a little intrigued. He was a voice of reason. I wasn't sure what to do with a person like this. What I felt at the time was rejection, and that was familiar to me, but it had always been in the context of anger, infidelity, or abuse. This healthy response was all new. Unfortunately, I was too unhealthy to do much with it besides wondering why he responded like that. So sad.

I did end up making one reasonably good choice—I wasn't going to see Nick anymore when he was drinking. That definitely limited our time together, so I decided to reconnect with some of my old friends I had put on the back burner while with him. One of them was a guy named Sean who had been part of the gang I partied with in high school. He was a nice guy, and we had liked each other but it never got intimate. He lived pretty close to where I was staying, and he lived even closer to Nick's parents' house. In fact, Sean knew Nick from school and there was no love lost between them.

I called Sean and he was excited to get together. He asked if I wanted to come out to his parents' house for lunch. We had a lot to catch up on and one of the things he shared was about his new job. He said he had a business dinner coming up and he would like me to go with him. He said it wasn't formal but definitely a dressy affair, and I had just bought a new dress for a wedding that would be perfect for this occasion. Sean was getting an award, and I think he wanted someone there to witness him getting it. This was exciting. Something I could look forward to. Definitely something I never did with Nick . . . but he couldn't find out.

The day I was to go out with Sean, Nick called and asked if I wanted to go to the Ale House with him that night. I made up some silly excuse and he sounded disappointed then tried again to talk me into going with him. I again apologized because I had something else going on. He became really angry, which I didn't expect. We had been clear about limiting time together, and I definitely wasn't going to the Ale House with him even if I had nothing else to do. He would be getting drunk, and I didn't want any part of it. Plus, his "friend" from the townhouse hung out there. The conversation ended with him hanging up on me. And I really didn't care.

I put on my beautiful dress, did my make-up and hair, and waited for Sean. When he arrived, he looked pretty awesome in his suit. We exchanged compliments and then took off. I would like to say that I had a wonderful time, but had not eaten all day, and it was an open bar. A year with Nick had increased my intake of alcohol and before I knew it, I was lit. I don't even have any memories of what happened other than waking up in Sean's car, and being afraid I embarrassed him. I realized pretty quickly I had gotten sick at some point, and that was a good thing. I waited for Sean till he came out of the event, so as not to embarrass him further. *Hmmm. Does any of this sound familiar? When will she get off the merry-go-round?*

Being the gentleman Sean was, he said I just drank too much and when I started feeling sick, I asked him if I could lie down for a while in his car. He promised me I had not embarrassed him, and no one had said anything derogatory about me. I could only hope he was telling me the truth. He pulled out his award, and was beaming. We hugged and I shared how proud I was of him as we drove back to my house. It was pretty late, so Sean dropped me off and waited till I got to the door. Fumbling in my purse for my keys, I turned and waved to him, mouthing "thank you" and he drove away. As I turned back to the door, I glanced down the opposite side of the street, and saw headlights coming on. I recognized them. It was Nick's car.

I frantically searched for my keys. Why didn't I pull them out in Sean's car? Finally, I felt my key ring, but Nick had already parked in front of the house. My hands were shaking so badly, I couldn't get the key in the lock. "Come on, Leslie, breathe! Find the keyhole!" Just as I felt the key slide in, my head was jerked back. My hair was being pulled so hard I fell backwards. And the beating began.

Today I believe God allowed me to be knocked out as soon as my head hit the ground, so as not to recall any of it. But the evidence was there when I woke up. The whole front of my dress was covered in blood. Nick was gone. My head was pounding. My stomach was aching. And my nose felt twice the size. I made it into the house and tried to call anyone I thought might be awake. No luck. The family I stayed with was gone for the weekend, but I also had to be careful who I shared this with. Then, I remembered Doug had given me his number. The last time we talked had been awkward and I definitely didn't think he would give me the time of day, but I knew I needed to go to the hospital. So, I called him.

I did not get the response I had expected. Not at all. He was all business, asking for the address, instructing me to leave the door open, and to stay awake. He came immediately and drove me to the hospital. Ironically, I had very little damage done to my face. A partially black eye and small cut on my lip. Most of the blood had come from my nose, and remarkably it wasn't broken. I asked the ER doctor why I couldn't remember what happened and they felt I must have hit my head against the brick step when he yanked my head back and it knocked me out. Because of that they did a CT of my head and also my chest and abdomen because of the bruising there. They assumed he must have kicked me several times. All the CT scans came back negative. As I was leaving, the doctor asked me if I wanted to press charges, and I said I just wanted to go home. Then he said what the surgeon who had operated on my arm had relayed to me, "You are a beautiful girl, and seem pretty intelligent. Why are you hanging with jerks like him?"

I realized he thought Doug had been the perpetrator. "Oh, no. It wasn't him. He's my friend. The guy that did this, I already broke up with and I am trying to end it."

The doctor shook his head and looked disgusted. "I hope this is the end. Next time he might kill you. Think about that."

Doug stayed with me the whole time, from clean-up to discharge. He drove me back to the house to get my clothes and then to his house because he didn't feel I would be safe anywhere else. I didn't argue. His parents were in Europe, and he kept me at his house for 6 days. It was a beautiful home in Potomac, and I stayed there even while he worked. I felt like a princess. I had called the people I was living with and told them I was staying with a friend for a while, housesitting. I couldn't let them see my face, until it healed.

Doug cooked for me, left meals for me while he worked, played games with me, we watched movies . . . and we talked. I had forgotten how easily we talked. It had been this way with Greg also. I didn't get it. Both of these guys had done more for me than I deserved.

On Friday, Doug came home with a one-way, non-stop ticket to Seattle, leaving on Sunday. He said he felt I needed to be with people who loved and cared for me, and my parents needed to know what I had been through. First, I thought he was crazy to spend that kind of money on me! Second, I thought he was crazy to think I would get any of what he expected from my parents. I definitely could not tell them what happened. I would just get the usual, "You must have done something to make him mad! You probably deserved it!"

He had been so thoughtful; I did decide to make the trip though. It would do me good to get away for a while even if it was under the pretense of wanting to see them. When I called my parents to tell them, I found out Aunt Ruby was there, and that was all I needed to hear. The evening of my trip, Doug took me to the house to get the rest of my clothes. I packed my suitcase and explained I needed to go home for a few weeks. They didn't suspect anything was unusual and then Doug drove me to Dulles Airport.

He made me promise I would keep in touch and asked me to call him frequently. He said he would be glad to pick me up from the airport when I came back home, and after that, we could see where our friendship/relationship was heading. I hugged him and whispered, "Thank you so much, Doug. You're an angel." I pulled back, and he kissed me. It was a very deep and passionate kiss. I didn't necessarily want it to end, but it had to. We hugged again, and I was off to my gate. I looked back once, and waved. He was still watching me.

Then that *voice*. That ever-present *voice,* whispering in my ear —*he's not for you, forget it.*

I never saw Doug again.

6

Another Miss

The plane was practically empty. It was a 747, and had three seats on each side and a row of 4 in the middle, and only about 10 passengers on the whole plane. I guessed there weren't many people who wanted to take the "red eye." A non-stop flight to Seattle meant a 5-hour trip. A lot of time to think. After we gained altitude, my thoughts went to how screwed up my life had been. I was all confused. Confused about what to tell my parents, confused about Doug, Nick, Greg, Shang, and most of all . . . me. I was 22 years old and had no understanding of how to make life goals, short or long term. No understanding of what a healthy relationship looked like. And no understanding of how to make anything any better. The weight of it all was unbearable. So, I did what I usually do, I dismissed it. Stuffed it. Buried it.

Almost simultaneously, the cabin darkened, and they began showing a movie. A stewardess was taking orders for drinks, and I had already decided I was going to take advantage of that benefit. *To help me sleep.* She surprised me when she stopped and handed me a soda with a mini of vodka. She smiled and said, "Compliments of the man over there." She nodded to the aisle of seats on the opposite side of the plane. I sat up and looked over and noticed a young man in a Navy unform. He held up his glass, flashed a smile and nodded at me. I returned the nod and mouthed, "thank you." He looked about my age and seemed friendly, but I wasn't looking for anything else on my plate right now.

Two more drinks came my way, and eventually so did he. He was very friendly and introduced himself as Glenn and asked if he could join me. I appreciated him taking the outside seat, leaving some space between us, and we exchanged pleasantries for over an hour. I felt myself begin to nod off, and told him I needed to get some sleep. He excused himself and I immediately stretched out on all three seats, and passed out.

I woke up with the stewardess telling me I needed to fasten my seatbelt. We hit some turbulence, and I was grateful for the reminder. She also brought us breakfast. After drinking on an empty stomach, I needed sustenance. I glanced over at Glenn. He was looking at me, and waved again. He seemed nice and gestured that he would like to come join me again. Nodding in agreement, my head went straight to where this might be going. Maybe just someone to talk to while on a long flight.

He shared he was on leave and going home to visit his parents in Bremerton, near Seattle. I shared I was going to see my parents as well, and they lived in Edmonds. That led to him asking if I would like to get together with him while I was in Seattle. During our conversation, the sun began to rise, and emerging in the opposite window was the most incredible sight. It was Mt. Rainier. And we were fast approaching it. It towered over the clouds like something imagined! I had lived in Seattle years ago, and had witnessed its grandeur often when we drove down Route 5, but this was a first. I was dumbfounded by its beauty. Glenn asked me if I had ever been to the park, and I told him, once, with my dad and brother. I stared at that mountain until we began to descend, and it was out of sight. Now there was nothing but clouds and rain.

After we landed, he helped me with my carry-ons, and I gave him my parents' phone number. I didn't know what they would think, but knowing my dad, he would definitely be all in for me going out with a Navy man. I didn't know if he would really call me, and I wasn't sure I cared, at this point. My head was still swimming from all that had happened, and how quick this decision to come here had been.

My reunion with my parents was good, and seeing Aunt Ruby and Reeshie again were the best. I shared nothing with my parents about the last few months, but found myself in Aunt Ruby's room late that night telling her everything. She was my rock. After everything had spilled out, I mentioned Glenn, and she thought it would be fun for me to hang out with someone who was a nice guy "for a change." And the next day, my parents agreed.

Let's break. Now none of my family had met Glenn, but were encouraging me to date him. Is there something wrong with this picture? Even though they knew little about the history with Nick, they surely knew about what I had been through with Shang, yet no one—not one of them— ever thought to tell me to take a break from men, and get to know—me. Just take a break and learn a few things about who Leslie is. So, I didn't.

Two days later, Glenn called and asked if I would like to go with him to see Mt. Rainier. I offered to make a picnic lunch, and he offered to bring a cooler of drinks. Aunt Ruby helped me make some fried chicken, deviled eggs, and potato salad. It was a feast. When Glenn came, I introduced him to my family, and we were off. I think I half expected he was going to bring a cooler of wine or beer, but he surprised me with sodas. We had an awesome day, and he knew of the perfect place for a picnic—right in front of a waterfall. I was in heaven!

We hiked through the park most of the day and when he took me home, he walked me to the door. To my shock, he requested to speak to my dad and asked if I could come visit him in Bremerton and stay for the weekend with his parents. He wanted to take me to see the USS Missouri, the ship where the WW II peace treaty was signed, and he wanted me to be with him for the "turkey shoot" he was participating in on Saturday night. Earlier at the park, we had talked about visiting him, but I didn't think it was a serious invitation. It required me to take the ferry over to Bremerton, and he would pick me up and take me to his house. I hesitated and said I wasn't really keen on seeing turkeys being shot, and he and my dad busted out laughing. My dad quickly explained, and then volunteered I was a pretty good pool player. So, that weekend, I got packed up and Dad took me to the ferry. It was about an hour's ride to Bremerton and Glenn was waiting for me.

His parents were very sweet, and reminded me of a lot of folks in Crisfield. Very down to earth and their house even smelled like my granny's house—a lot of baking and home cooking. That day we went and toured the ship, and then he took me to a beautiful beach off Puget Sound, and we sat and talked for a while. His mom prepared an awesome dinner that night, and afterwards we watched TV. I felt so relaxed and comfortable. The next day was just as nice, and Glenn and I just hung out on their porch with his parents.

That night was the turkey shoot, and Glenn and I were partners. I had not played in a long time, but he was so good, he made up for my mistakes, and we ended up winning! There was a monetary award and Glenn donated half of it to a local charity, and told me we would go out on the town with the rest of it. That night, we snuggled on the couch and watched a movie after his parents went to bed. And then he kissed me. And we kissed for a really long time. Nothing else. Just kissing. No pressure. And it was really nice.

The next day, he borrowed his parents' car and took me back on the ferry. He told me he knew exactly how to spend the winnings from the turkey shoot. So, we went to see a new Barbara Streisand movie, *A Star is Born*, then went to the coolest Japanese restaurant for dinner. Glenn was so easy. Reminded me a lot of Greg. During dinner, I had a thought flash through—I couldn't mess this up like I had with Greg. He was such a nice guy, and a Navy guy, at that. Dad would approve.

The next day he called and asked if he could take me to the Seattle Center, where the 1962 World's Fair had been. And then we would go dancing afterward. I loved to dance, and I had not seen the Center, so I was excited. He said he would pick me up the next day, and plan on spending the day with him.

First he took me to the Pike Place Market. I was there as a student when I was in 8th grade. Our art teacher took us there to draw. It was awesome to see it again, with all the fresh seafood and produce. Then we went up to the top of the Space Needle and had lunch. It was so cool. As it slowly rotated you could see all of Seattle and Mt. Rainier, too. Then he took me to the *Laserium* at the Pacific Science Center. It was mind-blowing. You lay on the floor in this huge dome-shaped building, and they did a laser show to some awesome rock songs—like Pink Floyd. It almost gave you a buzz just watching it. Then we had another awesome dinner before we went dancing. And the dance venue was huge! Not a dinky little bar, but a huge dance floor and light show. We only had a couple of drinks that night. In fact, I noticed we had hardly had any alcohol at any of the places we had gone together. And I didn't miss it. *Interesting.*

When Glenn took me home that night, I could hardly believe how much fun I had experienced. Completely relaxed with this guy, feelings had started forming. As we sat in front of my parents' house, I felt like I had to pinch myself on how lucky I had been to meet him. But this would be the first time we talked about his assignment. And the fact that he would have to leave in 2 days. He had just been assigned to the USS Eisenhower, an aircraft carrier that had just been commissioned and it was stationed in Norfolk, so that was good news. It would mean a 3-year stint, and he knew little about where he might be deployed. I went from feeling on Cloud 9 to sitting in the dust. I had seen what Dad's assignments had done to my mom, and I didn't want any of that. Heck, I knew what it had done to me, and did I want that in my future? I felt the brakes grinding down to the floor. Glenn saw the look on my face, and tried to backpedal, talking about how often we could see each other if I could get to Norfolk. But a switch had flipped, and I felt like I just needed to say goodnight.

He walked me to the door, and asked if we could get together the next day. I told him to call me but was already forming an excuse in my mind. He kissed me goodnight and it was as wonderful as always. That night was the first time since I had been home, I visited Dad's bar. And I went back several times.

The next day, I decided to spend time with Glenn, and we had fun just hanging out at a mall, and had another great dinner. But it was different. I felt it. He felt it. And we didn't talk about it. He just sounded sure I would come see him in Norfolk, and gave me his contact information. Since I had no home base yet, I really didn't have a number to give him. He was leaving the next day, so when he walked me to the door that night, he lingered longer than usual. I thought he was going to tell me he loved me, but those words didn't come.

I have wondered over the years if it would have made a difference if Glenn had said he loved me that night, but alas, I will never know. We kissed good-bye, and I went straight downstairs to my room. I listened for the TV to be turned off in the family room, a sign my parents had gone to bed. Then I hit Dad's bar again. And I hit it hard. That was a nightly thing until I went back to Rockville, the following week.

I purposely shared in detail all the wonderful things Glenn and I did together so you could see how I never even thought about a drink while we were dating. How sexually innocent our time was . . . and that was ok, too. I had been given a taste—as I had with Greg—of a life that was healthy. A life that was promising. A life that maybe I had been created to experience. One that didn't include trauma . . . and pain . . . and regret. A life I had never known. But trauma bonds are hard to break, and I didn't even know I had them. It's hard to fix what you don't know is wrong.

I never saw Glenn again.

7

The End of Reason

I was experiencing a lot of mixed emotions before I left Seattle. Doug was going to be there when I got back home, and Glenn was going to be in Norfolk soon. But I didn't feel "attached" to either one of them. Both had been super sweet to me: kind, caring, doting, respectful, loving. What more could I want? But I wasn't capable of answering that. I only knew I didn't feel attached. I didn't even want to talk to either of them. I had called Doug the day before I was to fly out of Seattle, to see if he could pick me up from the airport. He said he was working and stated, with a little frustration in his voice, that if I had called sooner, he could have arranged to get off. That was followed by queries about why I had not been in touch with him earlier. Which was followed by me feeling irritated and just wanting to get off the phone. I think he felt that and asked if he could call me later, so I gave him the number and was relieved to hang up.

There was something about Doug that was so straight-forward, so to-the-point, so not-a - game-player, so . . .

*The word here is so . . . healthy. But I had no understanding of such an extraneous fact. To be around someone who was not playing any kind of mind-game, or who was not controlling, or manipulative was so foreign to me. This was the commonality between Greg, Doug and Glenn. It was a turn-off for me **because** it was so foreign. Outside my norm. Uncomfortable. I didn't know how to handle it. So, I didn't.*

I found myself irritated, almost angry, when I talked with him, so I decided I wasn't going to pursue anything with him. When he called later that night and said he had switched with someone from work, and could pick me up, I lied and said I already had a ride and would call him when I got back. I knew I wouldn't call, but it got him off the phone.

43

I talked to Aunt Ruby about all of my feelings, and she told me to follow my heart. I wasn't sure if I knew how to do that, but I promised her I would try. Before leaving Seattle, Dad had found a room for rent in The Washington Post that allowed pets. It was a 3-bedroom apartment, and I would share it with two other girls. I was thrilled to be taking Reeshie home, and the timing was good since my parents had said they wouldn't be able to keep her any longer.

I was also taking home a new pet. My brother had bought a female Guina pig just before I got here, and he was worried about how fat she was getting. That was settled one morning when there were 5 little pigs in his cage instead of one. The babies were about the size of your thumb. I immediately had a favorite. I named him Sebastion. He was solid black with one white spot on his back. I wasn't sure how I was going to get him on the plane. Dad had called the airport about transporting pets like that, but they told him it wouldn't be possible. I was attached to the little guy, so he was definitely going with me. He had grown to about the size of a Twinkie by the time I was ready to leave, so I snuck him on the plane in my purse. I wrapped him in a towel, and all was well until takeoff and landing, when he let out a squeal just like a real pig. I coughed incessantly during both occasions, and though I got a few inquiries from the stewardess, who asked if I needed some water—and some very strange looks from other passengers—the cover-up was successful.

Camelia picked me up from the airport and took me to my new address. The girls seemed nice enough, and told me I could move my stuff into the apartment the next day. When I moved out of Nick's place, I had put all my furniture in a storage unit. There wasn't a lot, so Camelia and I called some friends to help me move in. All went well, and Reeshie acclimated quickly to her new environment. It was so obvious how happy she was to be back with me. We had been inseparable prior to Nick. It had been hard for me to let her go, but most of my thinking back then didn't include a lot of common sense. She would have made a much better roommate than Nick did.

When Doug didn't hear from me after I got home, he called my parents, and they gave him my number. My roommates left me multiple messages that he had called, but I never returned them. The same thing happened with Glenn. I didn't have any guilt about it, I just didn't think either were good choices. At least not for me.

It was mid-July, and Camelia was registering for her classes, so I also registered for classes at Montgomery College. I figured this would be my last semester of gen-ed before being accepted into the nursing program. We celebrated that night by going dancing at a new bar she had discovered in College Park. They had champagne on Monday nights for 25 cents a glass. Sounded good to me, so we went. The band was awesome, and we danced a lot. Champagne was flowing and we were feeling good. There had been one guy, we had both noticed sitting at the bar, who only danced occasionally. When Camelia went up to get refills for us, she asked him to join us.

Both she and I were taking a rest, so when he asked, we turned down his requests to dance. He was very sociable and said he had just moved here from South Carolina and was attending classes at the university, majoring in history. Camelia and I shared that we were in school too, she to be a medical assistant, and me to be an RN. His name was Gil—short for Gillian—and he became my first husband. We never separated after that first night. He dropped out of school and moved in with me the following week. We married a year later.

Our relationship was rocky from the start. I thought he cheated on me during our engagement, but had no proof, so I ignored the feeling in my gut. Then after our wedding and honeymoon, I caught him making out with a girl in our car, with our wedding gifts still in the backseat. One year into our marriage, I got pregnant in my last year of nursing school. Both of us felt happy about it, but my dad talked us into waiting. "This is bad timing. Have a baby after you finish school. Not now. You need your education." Gil bought Dad's advice more than I did, but the decision was made by both of us to end the pregnancy. Things went downhill from there.

One weekend, a friend he worked with asked if we could help her pack some boxes in preparation for their move. She had become a dear friend to both of us, and we hung out a lot with her and her family. We met at their house on Saturday morning, and were busy packing boxes when another friend of hers, Sam, showed up. When he introduced himself to me, my breath caught in my throat. It was like one of those scenes from a movie. I was dumbstruck. He was not only handsome, but tall and very muscular—but most of all, as sweet as he could be. I could not recall ever having a response to anyone like that. Every time he smiled at me, I literally had to remind myself I was married. It got to be so uncomfortable, I asked Gil if I could wait in the car because we were pretty close to finishing anyway. And, of course, as luck would have it, Sam left at the same time, and came by the car to say goodbye. I was grateful Gil noticed nothing suspicious in me. Sure, I had been attracted to people in the past, but—*phew*—this was different. Fortunately, I was over it in a few days, and felt I had moved on. After all, we would probably never cross paths again.

About a month later, Gil wanted to see a new movie that had just been released about King Arthur, *Excalibur*. As we were standing in line, someone grabbed me from behind and whispered, "Surprise!" in my ear. I saw Gil smile, and put out his hand to shake with the person. It was Sam. I felt numb all over. He asked if he could sit with us, and Gil quickly agreed, and went first to his seat, so that left me sitting between him and Sam. Today, I could not tell you what the movie was about. On 3 occasions, Sam's hand rested on mine, followed by an apology. All 3 times it was like electricity zipped from my hand to my arm, to the rest of my body. I could hardly wait for the movie to be over. He and Gil talked about getting together after the movie, and I just hoped I wasn't going to be included in that scenario. If they did meet, I never knew about it, and didn't see Sam again for a while..

Gil and I struggled through another year, and after I got my RN, things got even worse. As a new graduate nurse, I had been asked to assist with a 2nd trimester abortion in the hospital where I was working. As a new nurse, I didn't think I had an option to refuse, but after what I had just experienced myself, I was not too excited about the prospect. It was as awful as I expected. And to make it worse, the baby was older than they thought, and alive when it was born. It only lived for about 10 seconds, but enough for me to feel physically ill. I asked the doctor if I could go home. I was a wreck for many days after that, and began to feel unexplained anger with Gil. Over the next several months, we both drank more and drifted further and further apart. Then an event took place that ended it for good. I found out he had been sleeping with a nurse I worked with. She was 10 years his senior, and the shock of it was paralyzing. I kicked him out the next day.

After a few months, it seemed he had ended it with her, and we tried to patch things up. But during a moment of intimacy—when he called me by *her* name—I knew we were done. Camelia and I started hanging out again, and going to dance clubs. The pain inside of me was unquenchable. I couldn't drink enough to make it go away. Going out was my only refuge.

One night we were in a lounge, and we had danced a bit already, but on my way back from getting another drink, I saw a familiar figure. It was Sam. He saw me, came to our table, and asked where Gil was. I gave him the short version of what happened, and asked if he would like to join us. He sat with us for a drink, and after we talked for a while, I asked if he would like to dance. He shook his head, leaned over and kissed my cheek, and said he couldn't because I was "still a married woman." And then he left. Just like that. The attraction was definitely still there, but it was clear I was off limits.

Gil and I tried to put things back together a couple more times, but there was just too much water under the bridge. Too much betrayal. Too many lies. Too much pain. With all the agony I had already endured in my life, the death of my marriage was the worst yet.

I share these details—and I will share more from my relationships that followed—because I was entering into a new type of trauma. And I want you to understand how this new root was being grafted into all the other traumas I had experienced in my life. This was Betrayal Trauma. I talked about it in The Making of an Orphan *and how it had affected my mother. Well, now it was my turn. My mom experienced it multiple times with both her husbands. And my experiences seemed to be with every man I had chosen. Notice, I didn't say every man I had a chance to be with. You have met some of the excellent choices I passed by. Had I chosen them, I wouldn't be writing this book to hopefully help others not make the same mistakes I made. Or to help those who might be relating, learn why they made their bad choices, so they don't do it again.*

I had suffered betrayal in every one of my intimate relationships. But I held marriage as something different. Certainly not because I had witnessed a faithful marriage with my parents. But I needed to believe marriage would make a difference in my life. Something special. Something sacred. But the pain from the betrayals in my marriage relationship only caused me to turn cold. Desperate. Angry. Rebellious. Neglectful of all I believed was important. What very few boundaries I once had were now tucked away. I was in an all-out war to destroy myself. Because, after all, I must not deserve anything good. Things were about to get really bad. My unhealed traumas were going to take me to some darker places than I had ever been.

And I heard the voice in my head again, the one I had heard after that event at the party. The one telling me Greg, Doug and Glenn were no good for me. The one that seemed to agree with every negative thought I had, and every destructive thing I did. A voice that was becoming more prevalent. And more dangerous. And worse . . . I was listening.

8

Racing with the Devil

I experienced the next few years as if they were happening to someone else. In and out of relationships. Drinking more. Escaping more. Trying to bury my feelings. I didn't want to feel anything anymore. After the divorce from Gil, I stopped caring about almost everything. I even took Reeshie to Crisfield, to live with Aunt Ruby. I felt she would be happier with her than with me.

I felt nothing anymore. Numb. Helpless. Hopeless. The only thing I felt any sense of satisfaction with was my work. I loved being a nurse. So, I buried myself there. I volunteered for doubles any chance I could get. When I had a terminal patient, I stayed with them—no matter how many hours it took for them to pass—because I didn't want them to be alone. I knew what that felt like, and it wasn't fun. Yep, I stayed at work as many hours as I could get away with, because when I wasn't at work . . . I was alone. Deeply. Darkly. Alone. And when I was alone, I was in pain. And when I was in pain, I was forced to look for ways to numb it. Ways to reduce the force from the tsunami-like waves of anguish that tormented me. Finding parties where I could drink away the emptiness inside . . . and forget what a failure I was.

And something new had raised its ugly head—as if I needed anything else in my basket of goodies. I had a lot of friends at work who would invite me to their baby showers. And lately, it felt like I wasn't able to attend them. I didn't know why, but there was this overwhelming sadness, to the point of tears, every time I tried to go. So, I stopped trying.

In addition to that, it seemed I couldn't hold a baby anymore without that same sadness. I discovered this phenomenon when a position became available in our maternal/baby unit. I had waited three years for this opportunity. It was the first excitement I felt about anything in a long while. My desire to work in OB was finally going to be realized. But when I took the tour and saw all the babies in the nursery, that same paralyzing sadness overtook me, and I had to leave the tour before I burst into tears. I ended up turning down the position, which shoved me further down the dark hole I felt I lived in now. I didn't understand any of this, and it seemed no one I shared this with understood either. I had always loved babies. I had wanted 12 kids of my own. I had babysat for a family with a dozen kids when I was 14, and loved it! I just loved kids. So, all this was inexplicably confusing to me. I was clueless.

This whole baby thing just added more weight to my already heavy, guilt-tripped life. My dance dates became more frequent, and my drinking became more toxic. I was in a constant state of *numb-the-pain.* Any way I could. With anyone I could. With any substance I could. I felt hopeless to get myself out of this dark cavern.

Days turned into weeks, and I felt lonely, lost, and scared about my future. There was only so much work I could do, without earning too much overtime, but the overtime I had accumulated was a chunk of change. On a particularly lonely night, I started thinking about what things in my life had made me happy. Immediately, I thought of the horses. Could it be possible that I could buy a horse now? The idea was incredibly exciting. I knew a girl from high school who had her own farm, a bit of a hike for me, but I knew she would be able to guide me. So, I decided to drive out to her place.

Donna had several horses of her own, and she taught lessons. She happened to know of three horses that had been abandoned on a farm, after the owner went bankrupt. It was a mare and her two foals, a 2-year-old colt and a 1-year-old filly. The mare was a buckskin quarter horse, the filly was a strawberry roan, and the colt was solid black with a white blaze. All for the unbelievable price of $650.

She took me out to the farm, and I soon learned why the price was so cheap. All of them were very thin, having been left there in the middle of winter with no food other than field grass. They were very tame, beautiful horses, and I bought them on the spot. Donna helped me find a farm close to my house where I could board them and after I was able to put some weight on the foals, I quickly decided to sell them so I could concentrate all my attention on the mare. Her name was April Drizzle, and she was a registered quarter horse. Very seasoned and so sweet.

The only problem with having a brood mare was when they go into heat, they can become quite moody. And it often happens in the summer season. Sometimes I could ride her and sometimes she was obstinate. She was more than willing to eat my carrots and apples, but getting on her back was not going to happen during her season.

Buying these horses was the first good thing I had done, just for me, in years, and I loved every minute of it. Anytime I wasn't working, I was on the farm, riding. It was a 500-acre farm with lots of wooded trails. My full attention was on April and the incredible feeling of freedom I felt when we were at a full gallop, on an open field, feeling the wind and her mane in my face. Life was finally feeling good.

***

Almost a year had passed since my divorce, and I ran into Sam again. This time he was more than happy to dance with me. I was surprised at how thrilled he was to see me again. We began to date. He took me to nice places and brought me flowers and other special gifts. He was kind and sweet in every way. But I longed to feel his arms around me. To know he wanted me as more than a friend. To feel desirable. But . . . *woe is me* . . . it was a replication of Greg, and Doug, and Glenn. Kisses on the cheek. Hugs at my door. Never coming in for a drink. I could hardly believe it. The *voice* in my head kept saying, *this is happening all over again. This isn't love. He doesn't want anything but friendship.* What had become of all the breathless moments I had in his presence? All of it started dwindling. Another nice guy who was only interested in me as a friend. It was just my luck.

Weeks passed like this. I started making excuses when he called. I was not going to waste any more time on a "friendship." I needed to find a real relationship. I started going out more with Camelia and stopped going to the farm as much. I had plenty of friends who liked to go dancing, but Camelia was always my first choice. We hung out at places in Gaithersburg now, because DC was too far to drive—especially after drinking all night. The place we frequented the most had a chef who always brought out the food Camelia and I ordered. His name was Donny, and he flirted with me every time we came in. One night he asked me to hang out with him after the restaurant closed. And, yes, this was my next disaster. Without going into a ton of detail, let's just say he was another Nick.

The drinking led to the angry outbursts, that led to the slaps, that led to the punches. I wasn't even able to see the contrast between what I had with Sam and what I was experiencing now. I was too busy trying to "fix" his drinking . . . and him. I was certain if I could just make him happy, the drinking would stop . . . and so would the beatings. Yes, I lived in a world of make-believe. Instead of the hero riding in on his white horse to rescue the damsel in distress, I was going to ride in on my gray donkey and rescue the poor, sick, sad knave who didn't care one bit if I was dead or alive. Earning love. Earning attention. I was always trying to earn something in the relationship. I didn't feel worthy to just have it offered to me.

So, let's look at some things. This is called magical thinking. Trying to fix what wasn't right in the family of origin. This very unhealthy view of love was a learned behavior. As a child, I was always trying to earn my parents' love and attention. If you read The Making of an Orphan, *you know the silent treatments, the lack of parental attention and care, the belief I could never do anything right, the lack of physical care. All of these were part of the training ground leading me to believe the only way to get real love was to earn it. All that happened to me in that book had laid the groundwork for the life choices I was making now. They were not based on truth, but based on trauma responses.*

These were not all "little t" traumas. There were several "big T" traumatic events. A "little t" trauma is often considered ego-threatening because the person is left feeling helpless. They are sometimes minimized by others, and the victim is left feeling they have over-dramatized or over-reacted to what they are feeling inside, and so they try to dismiss it, or avoid it by rationalizing their feelings. This can often lead to feelings of shame and a desire to stuff the feelings associated with the trauma. The exasperating part is what may be fully traumatic to one person, may not be "a big deal" to another who has been raised in such an environment. It's their norm. But it's also denial. Some examples of "little t" traumas are financial issues, divorce, physical accidents, legal issues, job loss, infidelity, relationship loss and the loss of a dearly loved pet.

A "big T" trauma is something that could range from physical or sexual abuse to a natural disaster. Whatever the situation, the person is left feeling powerless to have changed the outcome. They feel helpless and often hopeless. There is a degree of avoidance in these situations also, but to the extent where the person avoids life in general, and becomes isolated and non- communicative. These types of traumas can be life-changing in their outcomes, if the person does not seek resolution through counsel and therapy. Examples are car accidents, sexual assault, domestic violence, a natural disaster, certain types of death, repeated betrayal or infidelity.

So, if we take all the unresolved traumas from my childhood and add the adult-life traumas—the physical assaults, infidelities and betrayals, the event at the party I attended with Nick, the divorce, and the abortion—you can see how I had stuffed all of these traumatic events. Having never received any counsel or therapy, I made major life decisions based on emotion and feelings. The abortion, especially, went against every part of who I was as a person, as a woman, as a future mother. The event at the party had done a number on my self-concept. Feeling worthy of loving treatment was nearly impossible after that because I didn't believe I deserved it. I am going to dig deep into both of those later. But for now, I want you to see how all these traumas were affecting every choice I made. Every sick and unhealthy decision. My limbic system was stressed to the max. And I had no idea I even had a problem. After all, this was what "normal" felt like. This was my comfort zone. My noxious, pathetic, anemic comfort zone.

***

Well, all my efforts never changed Donny, so I went deeper into self-medicating. I wasn't spending as much time with April, and I completely tuned Sam out of my life. I didn't tell him I was doing that, I just made myself unavailable, except for an occasional phone call. I tried to keep Donny at a distance. Things had to change. I knew I needed to get back into my routine of going out to the farm, and forgetting everything else in my life. That had worked before . . . at least for a while.

I tried to go to the farm a couple days a week. One day, I took Camelia out to meet April. She had bought a fifth of vodka to drink later that night, and we had already downed a few drinks before hitting the road. I tried to talk her into riding, but after her harrowing scare with a runaway horse when we were teens, she said "never again."

(*Side note: You never, ever, never ride a horse after you have been drinking. No exceptions. You just don't do it.*)

We were feeling pretty good as we pulled into the driveway leading to the barn and outer pastures. I got out of the car, and saw April on the hill a few pastures away. As always, when she heard my voice, she came running to get her hugs and her carrots. I went to the barn and got her saddle and bridle, but, unfortunately, it was one of her "off" days. Every time I tried to put her blanket on, she side-stepped. I finally gave in, fed her the carrots, and let her go back out to graze. I was heading back to return the saddle, when Camelia noticed a beautiful pinto gelding in the field. I had never seen him before, and thought he must be new to the farm. I put down the equipment, and we started to walk up the hill toward where he was grazing. He looked up and saw us, turned, and began to walk toward us. He was gorgeous, with perfect confirmation. When he reached us, he nuzzled my pockets where I had kept the carrots for April. "Sorry, boy, they are all gone."

He kept nuzzling, and I got the impression that he wanted me to ride him. Like it was whispered in my ear. What could put an idea like that into my head? But it was there, and I was going to act on it. He followed me back to Camelia's car and allowed me to put on the bridle, but wasn't too keen on the saddle. So, with my typically thoughtful, and wise decision making, I decided to ride him bareback. He was a big boy, probably 16.5-17 hands, so I had to stand on the side of Camelia's car to mount him. I could feel his muscles tighten and it was obvious he wanted to run. And I was ready.

We took off at almost a full gallop, and I realized I had probably never ridden a horse as big as this guy. I had a fleeting thought about how angry I would be if someone came out here and decided to ride April without permission, but it exited my mind almost as fast as it came. We were running at a full gallop! He was such a powerful animal; I was completely lost in the excitement of the moment.

And then it happened. He spooked. And he bucked. And I went flying. In an attempt to catch myself, I reached out with my right arm to break the fall. But it wasn't the fall that got broken. Camelia saw it happen and drove her car over to where I was sitting. She asked me if I was ok. My arm was pounding, and I felt dizzy from the pain, though I had not hit my head. "It's my arm. I think it's broken."

Even though she was an emergency room physician's assistant, Camelia blew me off. "No, it isn't, Les! Try to move it."

I looked down at my arm, and attempted to lift my hand off my lap, and the only thing that moved was my shirt, about 8 inches down from my shoulder. It appeared there was a little stub moving under my t-shirt.

"Don't do that again, Les. I am going to get some help." She looked scared,

"Camelia, I need you to get the bridle off the horse and get it and the saddle back in the barn. I am worried about getting sued or something." I tried to move, and for the first time, I realized I was hurting in a lot of places. "Maybe leave the vodka with me. And see if the phone in the barn is working."

After she had left with the equipment, I upended the bottle and took a long swig. The only thing I could think of was how in the old West they drank big gulps of whiskey before the doc operated on them. I decided it must be a good pain killer, so I took another. Yep, things started to get numb, and I lay down in the grass and waited.

I don't know how long it took for the ambulance to get there. But they finally arrived and by the look on their faces, I knew I had a bad injury. The ride to the hospital was short, and after getting admitted to the ER, I waited to be seen. This was the hospital where I worked, and this was the ER I often floated to when the census was high. I knew I was quite drunk. I had only eaten breakfast, and then downed a third of a bottle of vodka.

The doctor who was on duty was, of course, one I knew well. "Well, Leslie, I hear you had quite the ride today. Were you really riding bareback?" He kind of had a smirk on his face, but not an unkind one. More of a "I can't believe how stupid you are" smirk.

I pointed to the screen across the aisle from where I was sitting. It was an x-ray of the humerus bone of someone's arm, broken completely in half. The two halves of the bone were actually sitting on top of each other. "That looks pretty painful." I felt sorry for the poor guy it represented.

"That's *your* arm, Les! You completely broke your humerus in half. And the worse news for you? I am going to have to set it, without giving you any pain medication because you have been drinking." He shook his head slowly. "I am so sorry, but it's going to hurt . . . a lot."

Well, that was the understatement of the year. But worse than that? I found out this kind of fracture does not allow for a cast. It must remain immobile, flat against your body, held there with a brace, while the matrix regrows. And that takes a long time. And of course, it was my dominant arm. Which meant decreased mobility in my activities of daily living. Which meant I would not be able to work. Or take care of my home. Or cook for myself. Nothing. It meant I would have to go live with my parents for at least 6 weeks. And nothing about that made me smile.

I feel it's important to explain how this time period became what I know today as my "lost years." Lost in the darkness. Lost in the loneliness. Lost in the tools I used to numb my pain. But more than anything, I saw this as the death of what I longed for the most as I was growing up—the hope that I would finally experience life the way I had dreamt of it. The happy and faithful marriage. Lots of kids. The nice house with a white picket fence. Growing old in that one house where my kids and grandkids would come and visit me. Yeah, that dream was dead and buried.

The important thing for you to keep in mind is that I had no idea how the events of my life had affected me. I didn't understand how over the years all the traumatic things that had happened to me were affecting my brain, which in turn affected my thinking, my feelings, and my behaviors. Not to be redundant, but again, until someone tells you there is something seriously wrong—you don't know. And I was ignorant of all of this. I only knew I was in pain, and I had to get rid of it—in whatever way I could. Of course, these were temporary fixes. Addictions in general are all ways we run away from our pain. Relationships. Alcohol. Drugs. Burying ourselves in work. Substances of all kinds. Escapes. Codependence at full throttle. And I was entering into my own Fast and Furious video—without the car. I had my own private Grand Prix taking place. And the whispering voice I had come to know so well?

It was encouraging me at every step.

9

Desperate Times Call for Desperate Measures

Moving in with my parents in Blacksburg, VA, a five-hour drive from my home, at 29 years old, well, it was a challenge, to say the least. It's probably a challenge for anyone who has lived on their own for any length of time. But for me, with the family history we had, it was way more than a challenge. It was torture. Please don't misunderstand. My mom did her best to take care of me, as she was able, and was attentive, when she was able. But her capabilities ran parallel to the mood she was in, which ran parallel to my father's moods. Just watching the interaction between them was triggering for me. I tried to stay away from them as much as I could, but with my right arm in an immobility sling, no capacity to drive, and on top of a mountain of pristine 5-acre estates, it was impossible for me to get far enough away. The things I usually turned to for comfort, I had to leave behind—both my horse and my dog. Of course, Reeshie was still with Aunt Ruby, but I could have used her licks and hugs. And alcohol would not be an option, because I sure didn't want to hear what nuclear blast that might set off if I drank.

In addition to my parents, my brother was here, too. And things with him were not what they used to be. Once upon a time, he had been my defender, and would confront both Mom and Dad on the way they treated me. But now, he seemed to join forces with Dad against me and Mom. An example of this was one evening we were watching TV, and my dad had just received a package with a new calculator he had ordered. I saw him show it to my brother and then this visual exchange between them. Then Dad handed me the calculator and asked me if I had seen one like it. I told him I hadn't, and he gave me a math problem to enter in it. It definitely didn't work like calculators I had used before and when I looked up to share that with him, I saw he and my brother giggling as they watched me trying to figure it out.

My heart sank in my stomach, as I felt all the old feelings rise—all the times Dad had made me feel stupid as a child when I didn't understand something. All the feelings of never being good enough. All the feelings of being in my younger brother's shadow. I felt the tears begin to well up and was determined not to let them see me cry, so I stood up and handed Dad the calculator. I choked out, "Hope you got a good laugh" and went upstairs. Six weeks of this was going to be nearly impossible to handle.

Before I left home, I had given both Sam and Donny my parents' phone number. Donny called a couple times to see how soon I would be coming back. He probably needed me to come home because he wanted money for rent or beer. Sam called the third week I was there, asking if he could come visit me. He said he had already called the Blacksburg Airport, and could fly his plane down and spend the whole day, and then fly back that evening. I should have been excited, but instead, I had a ton of mixed feelings about him meeting my family. I just never knew what might be said. I told him I would talk with them and see what a good date might be.

Their response surprised me a bit. They seemed genuinely excited about having him come visit. Dad was especially interested in seeing his airplane and "maybe getting a ride in it" which thoroughly concerned me. The thought of him and Sam alone and talking—and possibly about me—was just scary. Dad had no filter when it came to giving people my resume of failures. I gave Sam a date for a couple weeks out, so my arm would be closer to full healing, and decided to be excited about it. At least, I would have a whole day with no parents.

The next two weeks seemed to descend even deeper into the life I had escaped from with my parents. Dad's put-downs. Mom's silent treatments. The triangulation game with both of them wanting me to take sides. It was beginning to really take a toll on me, and I was feeling desperate to get away. Just a few days before Sam was to visit, Camelia called me just to see how things were. I told her what I was dealing with, and how badly I wanted to get out of here. She suggested something I had not thought of—take a bus back home and she would pick me up. What a brilliant idea! Prior to that suggestion, I thought I was at the mercy of my dad's availability to get me back home. But now, I had an option. We got off the phone and I immediately called the bus station, and found out there was a bus that went straight through to Silver Spring and Camelia agreed to pick me up. My only concern was being a week out from when the doctor had said I could travel with the sling, but I would take the chance. Anything to get away from here.

My next issue was Sam. I wasn't sure how to break that news to him, and didn't want him to get upset, but also wasn't willing to stay just so he could make the trip. I called him that evening and lied about the reason I was coming home early—a doctor's appointment. He offered to fly up early and bring me back on his plane, but nothing about that was appealing to me. Not with an arm that wasn't working—not even part time. I promised him I would call after I got back home, and then I decided to break the news to my family.

Dad was fine with it, but Mom was upset with me. She had made plans for us to do some shopping together and, as usual, took my decision as a personal assault—as if I had planned it—just to hurt her. Some things never change. Dad said he would take me to the bus station the next day, and it was a Saturday, which worked perfectly with Camelia's schedule. I was so excited at the thought of being free from all this.

The next day, I packed up and, as expected, my mom was doing the silent treatment, and would not even say goodbye to me, and my brother was off with his friends. So, Dad drove me to the bus station, and wished me luck. He asked me to let him know what the doctor said, and then he drove away. Just left me there, in the parking lot, with my bags. Didn't wait for my bus to arrive, or help me get my bags into the station, or be sure I was ok getting on the bus. I couldn't help but remember all the times as a teenager, when I would sit on the dock, as he was heading out to sea for duty. I would stay there and watch till his ship was out of sight, crying my eyes out at how much I would miss him. And today, I got left, with my arm in a sling, in a parking lot . . .

Nope. Some things never change.

Camelia was waiting for me when the bus arrived, and had the awesome idea of heading to Annapolis. The weather was mild, unusual for July, and the idea of hanging out by the water was very appealing. She wanted to take me to a new bar she had discovered, right on the docks. I was still wearing my sling, so I had to be really careful in crowds. She suggested we sit outside where there would be less people, so we got an outside table on their patio. She ordered a new drink for us that she had recently tried—a Long Island Iced Tea. When the waiter brought them, they came with a warning from him—drink slowly because they go down easy, but they have a kick. To avoid arguments, and because I didn't want to slow down the healing process in my arm, I had avoided alcohol altogether while at my parents. But tonight, I felt like I had been freed from a cage, and I was going to enjoy this drink. The waiter was right. They went down easy. Real easy. I didn't notice the alcohol at all, so I ordered a second one for both of us. Camelia was being more reasonable than me about her drinking since she was driving. I just wanted to forget the last five weeks of memories that had been triggered with my parents.

The next thing I knew, I was feeling no pain, and Camelia was close behind. We decided to take a walk along the docks. As we were coming around the opposite side from where we started, we ran into a group of guys, standing around, talking, and drinking beer. One of them said hi to me, so we stopped. He seemed nice enough, and one of his friends started talking with Camelia. He introduced himself as Kyle, and his friend was Billy. It quickly became apparent, they wanted to hang out with us, and asked if we could go pick up some more beer. Camelia was willing, so they said goodbye to their friends, and we walked back to the car. I sat in the back with Kyle. He asked about my arm, and I explained how stupid I had been trying to ride bareback on a horse that wasn't mine, while drinking. We both laughed and he shared some of his "stupid" escapades. He was really easy to talk to. Maybe too easy in my state of mind, and it wasn't long before we were making out. Camelia found a store that was still open, bought the beer, and then they invited us back to their place.

It was a typical bachelor pad, and they shared it with another of the guys they had been with on the docks. We played some cards and then watched a movie, and ended up spending the night there. I had not considered Sam even once during this time. In fact, I didn't consider much of anything besides the relief I felt from the alcohol, and the distraction a new relationship might bring me. The triggers and depression I had felt at my parents', were now shoved back down inside, where I liked to keep them. Where they belonged.

As Camelia and I were driving home the next day, both of us were excited about our new boyfriends. She really liked Billy, and I felt the same for Kyle. And both of them wanted to see us again. It was about an hour's drive to my place, and as soon as Camelia had helped me get my stuff into the apartment, the phone rang. It was Kyle. He and Billy were inviting us back that night to hang out. It was a no-brainer for either of us, so we decided to meet them that evening.

Pretty quickly we discovered the reason they wanted us to come to Annapolis was because neither of them owned a car. But that was okay because both of us did. Also, neither of them had full time jobs at the present time—they were construction workers—and were hoping to find some work farther away from Annapolis. But that was okay because Camelia and I both had jobs. In fact, that night Camelia bought the beer for everyone, because they had no money. Then Camelia found out Billy had to move out of the house because he couldn't afford the rent, and Kyle would probably have to as well, because the rent would increase for just 2 people. Well, none of that was a problem. Why? Because they could just move in with us! Neither Camelia nor I had roommates, so we could just move these great guys in with us, and solve all their problems.

A quick break. If it sounds like I am being a bit sardonic in the above paragraph, well, I am. Anyone reading this with half a brain can see that these guys were not good choices—not for boyfriends. But if you remember from The Making of an Orphan, Camelia had her own baggage full of unresolved traumas, and her codependency was running as rampant as mine. Plus, a new one had been added to her bag. I found out soon after the guys moved in with us, she had just had another abortion. You may have remembered reading about her first experience when we were in high school. So, both of us were on the run. We were both desperate for distraction. Neither of us considered anything other than a new and exciting relationship that would numb our pain for a while. We were willing to support them, if in exchange, they became our distraction. Codependency + buried traumas = unhealthy decisions. And we were about to make a ton of them.

So, we moved both of them into our respective homes. And three weeks later, Camelia and Billy were witnesses to Kyle's and my marriage. Yes, you read that correctly. Three weeks later. We were all feeling pretty buzzed before we got to the courthouse, and afterward we went to Camelia's apartment, and kept the party going.

We all got too drunk to drive home, so we spent the night at her place, and the next day, moved the party to my condo. It was August, and Camelia's birthday was the next day, so we went out to eat for a champagne brunch at a local hotel, and then picked up some more liquor and beer to take back to my place. Almost as soon as we got in the door, Camelia and Billy made their announcement that they were going to get married the following week. And the dual celebration began. We were all feeling pretty good and watching a movie, when Kyle said he was going to take a shower. And I decided to change my clothes. Then the phone rang. It was Sam.

"Hey, Les! I was wondering if you would like to go out to dinner and see a movie tonight? I have missed seeing you, and thought since you have been home for a few weeks, you might be pretty much healed up by now. What do you think?"

Wow, this one was going to be interesting. "Hi, Sam. That sounds like it would have been great, but I got married yesterday . . ." *Long pause.*

"You what?" *He sounded incredulous. Not angry. Incredulous.*

"I got married yesterday."

"But you just left your parents' house a few weeks ago. How long have you known this guy? Were you with him while we were dating?" *A reasonable question.*

"No, Sam. I just met him in Annapolis the day I came home. Like three weeks ago." *Another long pause—longer than last time.* "Are you still there, Sam?"

"You just met this guy three weeks ago and then married him? You don't even know him!

You don't know anything about him! What were you thinking?" *Now he sounds very irritated.*

"I don't know how to answer that. Yes, it was only . . ."

Cut me off before I could finish. "Didn't you know I was in love with you, Leslie? Didn't you know I wanted to marry you? I even bought a ring! I thought we were building something. I don't understand."

Now I was feeling irritated. "Sam, you never even tried to kiss me. It was always a kiss on the cheek. You never wanted to come into my apartment and have a drink or watch a movie with me. It felt like we were just good friends. Nothing more. What did you expect?"

"I was respecting you, Leslie!" He sounded exasperated. "I wanted you to know I wasn't like the other guys you had told me you had been with. I wanted you to know our future would be so different than what you had been exposed to. I wanted you to know how much I loved you." *Another long pause.* "I wanted to marry you."

Shock would be a mild euphemism for what I was feeling. I had been completely clueless to his feelings for me. If he had shared any of that . . . if he had given me even a hint of his feelings, things could have been completely different. But now it didn't matter. I was with Kyle. And we were happy. We were going to build a life together. We were going to have a baby as soon as we could, because that had become very important to me. Sam was in the past now. "I am sorry, Sam. I just never got that impression from you, so I had to move on. I am sorry."

Another long pause. "Leslie, I am afraid you will be sorry. Very sorry. It will never last."

My irritation spilled out this time. "Well, Sam, that remains to be seen, and it's really none of your business. I am sorry." And I hung up.

At that moment, Kyle came out of the bathroom. "Who was that?" "Just an old friend. He didn't know I had gotten married."

"Oh, an old boyfriend?" He smiled, as if it was a joke.

"No, just a friend. He was nothing more than an old friend."

***

Yep, I married a guy I had only known for 3 weeks. Was I desperate? Absolutely. But not as much for a man as the need to fill a void. Actually, several voids. The death of the baby had left a huge hole in my soul, but I was not consciously aware of it. I knew nothing about post- abortion trauma or its after-effects on the mother. The death of my marriage had left another hole. Another place of betrayal. Rejection. Abandonment. All things I experienced as a child, a teen, and even as a young adult. Divorce equals failing. And for me, failing meant being a failure.

But the biggest void of all was the death of my dream. The one with the princess, the castle, and the knight in shining armor who would rescue her from all her woes. The one with the happy ending. The one where I would live happily ever after. I had no idea I had a deep-seeded desire to "fix" all that was wrong in my childhood. I didn't understand I was trying to make it all better. And if I could make it all better, I could finally forget how awful it had been.

So, I jumped at the first chance that presented itself, where I could possibly make that happen. The first guy who came along who could help me repair all the bad, and make the dream come true. I could fix him, mold him, change him into the person I knew he really wanted to be. I knew nothing about his past. Nothing of his family. Nothing of his habits. Nothing of his personality. All I knew was he liked to party—a lot. And I could party with him. And that meant I didn't have to think about anything else. I didn't have to think about what I had passed up with Sam. Or Greg. Or Doug. Or Glenn. I could live in the lie that I now had a husband—and that was almost like ownership. And we would have a baby, and then he wouldn't leave me. He couldn't leave me if we had a baby. We would be a family. And we would buy a house and have that white picket fence. And all would be well . . .

Denial can be a beautiful thing.

10

And the Walls Came Tumbling Down

"Humpty Dumpty sat on a wall. Humpty Dumpty had a great fall.
All the king's horses and all the king's men couldn't put Humpty together again." Mother
Goose Nursery Rhyme

Marrying someone three weeks after meeting them leaves a lot to learn about each other. I knew Kyle liked to party, but I didn't know he was an alcoholic. I knew he liked to do "speed", but I didn't know he was a cocaine addict. I knew his parents were divorced but I didn't know how severely abandoned and rejected he had been. How unattached he had been. How incapable he was of loving a wife and family—or even committing to a relationship. I didn't know any of his transgenerational traumas.

And he didn't know all my dirty little secrets either. My codependency was exactly what he didn't need as an addict, and an addict was exactly what I didn't need as a codependent. But it seemed I had this little radar on my head, and my message could be picked up from miles away, "Here I am. Please come abuse me. Please let me try to fix all your problems. Please let me screw your life up as much as you will screw up mine." Yep, that was my sign. My bright, fluorescent, blinking neon sign. And I was back in the same trap I found myself in so many times before—and I never saw it coming.

I thought maybe a new job would help me feel better. So, I applied and got a position in Oncology at the NIH in Bethesda. And I got pregnant almost immediately. I planned it and was successful. During my pregnancy, I learned a lot about this man I had married. He did not know how to be in a relationship. He didn't know how to be faithful. He didn't know how to be honest. But he was a hard worker. He got a job almost immediately after moving in with me, and went to work every day. And every pay day, he spent his whole check on beer, speed, cocaine, or crank (methamphetamine). He didn't ask me about the budget, or if his paycheck might help with it. It was *his* money, and he spent it the way he wanted. Thankfully, since I was a nurse with a great job, my paycheck paid our bills. But having a baby meant planning. My desire to buy a house meant budgeting. And learning about each other meant spending time together. He had no clue how to do any of these. My anxiety and stress levels were out of control, and it was showing in my pregnancy. I had to be hospitalized several times for pre-eclamptic symptoms.

Our son, Mike, was born in June, and due to a complicated birth, I had to stay in the hospital for almost two weeks. Mike also had tachypnea (elevated respirations) and was on antibiotics prophylactically. Kyle disappeared after the first few days. I had no idea where he went, but when I discovered my credit card was missing, and called to cancel it, I found it had been topped out. When I called the company to find out where it had been used, the report was shocking. Then it was crushing. It has been used at just about every stripper club in the DC area. This was my first wake up call.

Coming home with the baby was not the joy I thought it would be because I was never sure if or when he would come home from work. My mom stayed with me for the first few weeks, and he was pretty consistent to be home each night. While she was there, she talked to us about moving to Crisfield because there was a new prison opening close by, and Kyle could get a job there as a correctional officer and I could work in the hospital in Crisfield. She said she and Dad were moving to the Eastern Shore as well, and we would be close to each other. It sounded like a great plan, and Crisfield had always been my safe place. Aunt Ruby would be there, and I could have Reeshie back.

We gave notice to our apartment, put our things in storage, and went to stay with my parents in VA, while we house hunted. We found a house pretty quickly, but it wouldn't be ready for a few months. The real estate company had a trailer they used for situations like this, and I was excited to have Reeshie stay with us when we moved there. That's when I got the sad news my dear dog had died, and Aunt Ruby had chosen not to tell me because of the problems with my pregnancy, and with Mike, after he was born. It was crushing to think I would never get to see her again. Reeshie had been with me through a lot of dark times.

Kyle took some side jobs with his old boss back in the DC area during the week, while I stayed in Crisfield with our son. He was supposed to come home every weekend, but after the first 2 weeks, that started to slide. I realized the weekends he wasn't coming home were pay days, and I could only guess what was going on. But I kept my mouth shut to avoid arguments.

We finally moved into the house and began what I thought was going to be my fairy tale life. I learned very quickly how far-fetched my dream had been. Within weeks, it became apparent that Kyle needed to be in rehab, and after many threats and verbal battles, he finally agreed to go.

I feel it's important to explain a few things here. As hopelessly unhealthy as I was, you should know there were some newly added causative factors. Besides all the traumas from growing up, there were now the added traumas I mentioned earlier. Divorce, plus the abortion. A "rainbow baby" is a pregnancy that happens very quickly after a miscarriage or abortion. The deceased baby has left such a large void in the mother's psyche, she will often get pregnant immediately after the loss, or as soon as she can. And sometimes she discounts the possible health issues or emotional issues that have not yet been resolved from the death of the baby. The grieving process may not be complete. And the new pregnancy can cause many of those unresolved feelings to raise their ugly heads and cause even more issues.

In my case, I was going to have a rainbow baby AND a rainbow marriage. And none of my grieving for either had resolved. It had not even been addressed. Why? I didn't know I was supposed to grieve the aborted baby. If having an abortion was socially acceptable, why would I grieve it? And the failed marriage wasn't my fault. He cheated, and so it was over. Besides, everyone gets divorced nowadays.

I learned these lessons well. And if I said anything to my friends, regarding being sad about the abortion or the divorce, they told me to get over it and move on. Yep, I had stuffed all those feelings way down . . . way down, deep inside. And that voice (the one always right there to remind me what I needed to do) agreed I needed to keep them there.

So, Kyle got into rehab, and he seemed to be doing well. When it was time for me to be brought into his sessions, we both attended them to further his recovery. I learned about codependency for the first time—not how to heal from it, or what caused it, but the label. A group of behaviors I was to unlearn by going to Al-Anon. So I went, and I learned how to not enable Kyle anymore. How to stop trying to fix him. How to stop keeping his inventory. How to stop driving up and down the road on the nights he didn't come home, crying my eyes out— believing he might be dead—with my son in the back seat. I found going to meetings very helpful, and I had an awesome sponsor that kept my head on straight during the hard times. I learned a lot about how to disconnect from him, but not why I became a codependent in the first place. I didn't learn what it was from my past that had taken me to this location of insane living. I didn't learn what was missing in me that believed living like this was even remotely okay. I did learn, for the first time, a quote I would carry with me the rest of my life, credited to Albert Einstein, "The definition of insanity is doing something over and over again and expecting different results."

The impact of that truth would not reach its full potential in my life for many more years.

That was the first of Kyle's four rehabs. I am not going to go into all the details of what happened for the rest of our marriage. The redundancy with the other relationship failures I have already shared would be just that—redundant. But I will share a few life-changing events.

After rehab, I found out Kyle could not work as a correctional officer, because he had done a stint in jail for drugs. Never knew this. Didn't want to. He found a job, locally, working in construction. I began working at the hospital in Crisfield. For about 4 months, things went smoothly, and then the "dry-drunk" symptoms started. This is a term Al-Anon taught me, and it is defined as a person who isn't drinking but has many of the symptoms of when they do—trying to start arguments, irritability, dramatic exits, disappearing, etc. It was a possible warning sign he might relapse. And he did.

The next year was a repeat of the prior year. This time he left for five days, and he came back without his wedding ring. He said he sold it for cocaine. I insisted he get help. This time it was a 30-day residential treatment center. It was actually a relief to not have him around the house. But in my unhealthy state—it wasn't because things were so less stressful and so much more peaceful—it was because I actually knew where he was for 30 straight days. And that felt like safety. So, when he came home, our son and I prepared a very warm reception with a steak dinner and cake. It was a wonderful reunion. And I got pregnant again.

I was happy, but for him it was an "inconvenient" pregnancy. He said he couldn't handle another kid now, after just getting out of rehab. He said it would drive him back to drinking— that he needed time. Time I didn't have. I fought for the life I was going to end. I begged for my baby's life, but he was adamant and threatened to leave me. I tried for two weeks to convince him we could make it. I would keep the kids out of his way. He wouldn't have to be stressed by them. I would do the majority of the care. I was talking to a brick wall.

I went to my OB/GYN and begged her to tell me there was no heartbeat. No life. She assured me it was just a "clump of cells"—a definition with which I was most familiar. I believed her, and chose to go through with it, but this time, I requested they put me to sleep so I would not feel or remember anything. I did not anticipate the voice in my head—different from what I was used to. Softer, but with authority, telling me I was making a horrible mistake and to get up and run. But the pre-op medications had done their job well and I was unable to move, or even talk. The anesthesiologist just patted my arm when I tried to get his attention, telling me, in a few minutes, everything would be okay. The last thought I had before they put me to sleep was that nothing would ever be okay again.

When I woke in the recovery room, Kyle wasn't there. I didn't care. In fact, I didn't care if I saw him. My anger was palpable. I dressed, and they took me out to the waiting room in a wheelchair. When I saw Kyle sitting there, the explosive anger I felt was shocking. If I had had a gun, I would have shot him. He touched my shoulder. "Are you okay?"

I shrugged it off. "Don't touch me!" The nurse asked me if I was alright. "Please, just take me to the car." My gut felt empty, like something had been ripped out. I refused to let my heart expound on that thought. I sat in the back seat to avoid being close to him. He looked confused. I didn't care. That night I slept in Mike's room. Kyle never asked any questions, and I never offered any conversation. I didn't even know what I was feeling . . . except the anger and emptiness that was ever-present.

Things stayed that way for several days. I had the rest of the week off from work, and I did nothing but play with Mike. He was a very smart 2-year-old, and we spent hours putting together a Sesame Street alphabet track, reading books and making puzzles. I could not get enough time with him. I didn't even want him to go to bed at night. And I was clueless as to why.

Exactly five days after the abortion, on a Friday, I got a phone call from my doctor. She had received the pathology report and wanted me to know that it showed "products of conception," meaning the abortion had been successful. Then there was a long pause. "You also have an infection we need to treat right away, Leslie."

What? I had an infection that needed treatment? "What kind of infection?" I assumed it was from the procedure.

"It's Chlamydia, Leslie. We need to treat you and your husband ASAP. As a nurse, I am sure you are aware this is an STD."

Breathless, I thought, *Oh, yeah! I am fully aware! How long had I had it? Was this from his last disappearance? Then the real issue hit me. He had been screwing around on me, then coerced me to abort our baby!* My heart was pounding in my chest. I felt like I couldn't take a deep breath. This could not be happening. I had to get control. "Yes, of course. I didn't know. Please call in the prescriptions for us."

There was a long pause, "I am sorry, Leslie."

"Yes, I am, too. Very, very sorry." I hung up the phone as if I was in a dream. Ha! A nightmare was more like it. I felt panicked, but couldn't move. My legs went numb, and I collapsed in the chair next to me. Mike climbed up in my lap and hugged me. The tears started. They didn't stop for over an hour.

I got myself together as much as possible, put Mike in his stroller, and walked to the pharmacy. On the way, I tried to regurgitate all the happenings from his last disappearance. I had been going to Al-Anon long enough to not ride the roads anymore looking for him, but the worry had been ever-present. He had never stayed longer than a weekend in the past. This was 5 days. When he came home he looked as he always did. Pale, eyes sunken, appearing to have dropped 10 pounds. And this time he was missing his wedding ring. He told me he had sold it for cocaine—the instigating factor that made me demand he go back into rehab. But now I wondered if he took it off because he was hiding that he was married. So, he could be with someone else. So, he could have sex with someone else. The betrayal I was feeling was unimaginable. I had to end this marriage. It was never going to get better. Clearly, it was only getting worse. I had never had an STD in my life, and I had gotten one from my husband. What is that?

Then the voice began its usual tirade of accusations. "*That, my dear, is infidelity. He cheated on you, just like Gil did. You can't seem to keep a man loyal to you. What's wrong with you? And you can't leave him because you will be single, with a child. You will never make it on your own. You don't have what it takes to be a single mom. You need to just bite the bullet, and pretend all is well. After all, you married him . . .*"

That hated voice in my head. I despised the things I heard, but, at the same time, felt the words must be true. How could I raise a son by myself? He needed his father. I needed a husband. I needed the dream to be real. It was true, I had the marriage, the son, the house, and the white picket fence I had always wanted. But it certainly wasn't feeling the way I thought it would. I had just sacrificed another baby hoping to keep our family together. If nothing else, for that reason alone, I had to make this work.

I picked up the prescriptions and walked to Aunt Ruby's house. I had not told her anything about what had happened. She knew about his alcohol and drug use, and the disappearances, but not about the abortion. I needed some words of encouragement, and she never judged me. I knew I would get what I needed from her. Someone to confirm I was making the right decision. She loved my son, and I felt she would encourage me to stick it out. After all, that's what my family did. Good, bad, or indifferent. We just stuck it out.

***

Two more years passed, and nothing much changed. I developed a "whatever" attitude, qualifying it as a good Al-Anon head space. Indifference. Letting Kyle be Kyle, and not being controlled by it. Focusing on my son and me. I had transferred to a new hospital and Kyle had acquired a job there in maintenance. It felt like things were on an even keel for a while.

I even started seeing a counselor at the hospital for the codependency I was learning about in Al-Anon. He seemed like a nice guy, maybe a little friendlier than I expected. But it had been years—as far back as high school—since I had seen a counselor other than the rehab groups with Kyle. So maybe his attentiveness was normal. On the fifth visit, I was sharing my pain of learning about the infidelity following the abortion. I was tearful and he handed me a Kleenex. There was such a long pause, I looked up at him. He smiled. "Leslie, with your beautiful large breasts, I can't imagine any man seeking another woman." *What?* I was speechless. I was numb. I panicked.

"I think I am done for today. Thank you." I couldn't get out of the door fast enough. There had been several other times in my life when I felt as I did now: the hitchhiking incident, the time my father tried to kiss me, and the time at the party with Nick. Walking to the car, my breath came in short puffs. Heart pounding, hands shaking, I could barely get the key in the ignition. I felt as if I was going to pass out. Putting my head on the cold steering wheel helped me get some control back. What was I going to do? If I told the police, it would be my word against his. If I told anyone at the hospital, they wouldn't believe me. This guy had been there for a while. It was as it always was. Keep my mouth shut and pretend it didn't happen. But I made a vow that day. No more counselors. Ever.

✳✳✳

More time passed and I became pregnant again, this time with a baby I would keep, regardless of what Kyle wanted. But he seemed okay with the news. We started working on the extra bedroom to make it into a nursery. My son, Mike, would be a month shy of 4 years old when this baby was born. That felt very manageable for me. I had been working in Oncology at the hospital, and was moved to the float team to prevent exposure to chemotherapy. Kyle seemed to be holding down the maintenance job. I actually began to feel things were going to work out well.

I was very excited to hear from the doctor that they were now performing ultrasounds regularly during the first trimester. I would be able to see my baby at the first appointment. With great anticipation, I watched as the doctor scanned my belly, and zoomed in on the baby. I smiled with tears of happiness, as I saw the heartbeat, and saw my little baby jumping, with its tiny arms and legs. It looked like a little Teddy Graham! The doctor informed me the baby measured at just under 8 weeks. He printed out some pics for me, and I left the office full of joy.

But that joy was short lived. Driving the 30 minutes it took to get home, reality and truth began to pierce my memory. I became starkly aware this baby was the same age as those that I had aborted. My gut felt like it had hit the floor. I was crying so hard; I had to pull the car over. My chest was heaving with the recognition of what I had done. The lies I had been told. The lives I had taken. The reality of it was in my face, and it was a tough pill to swallow. This was a door opening—an important door—but not one that I was ready to walk through yet. So, I did what I always did. I swallowed it. By the time I got home, I had filed all that pain in a new box of memories and sadness. A new file to add to all the others. A file labeled: "To be continued . . ."

***

During my second trimester, I met another nurse who was also pregnant, and who seemed to be on every floor I was assigned to. That was odd. The chances of 2 float nurses being assigned to the same floor on a regular basis were pretty slim. After several times of noticing this, I finally asked her, "Don't you find it odd that we are always assigned to the same floor? I am getting paranoid that administration is watching us or something!" I chuckled with a laugh that owned no humor. I really was in a quandary.

Her name was Lonnie, and she smiled at me with much kindness and assurance, "No, I don't find it odd. I think there is a purpose behind it." That felt incredibly mysterious. But it was the beginning of a friendship I would never have expected in a hundred lifetimes.

Lonnie and I were only weeks apart in our due dates. We both worked 12-hour shifts, 3 times a week, and she was a great storyteller. Eating lunch together was always a curiosity for me. Her stories centered around her faith and all the things she felt Jesus had done in her life. Things that were nothing short of miracles. I would listen, mostly in disbelief at first, since I knew nothing like that had ever happened in my life. And it never would.

After a couple months, she finally asked me if I wanted to hear about how to have a personal relationship with Jesus. "You only have to believe He came to save you from your sins and give you everlasting . . ."

I held up my hand in front of her face before she could finish. "No thank you, Lonnie. My dad is an atheist, and he has shown me many things about the Bible that are questionable. He even believes Shakespeare wrote the Bible, and he showed me all the places in the Bible where it seems possible. No, I am not interested in hearing about that. I do love to hear your stories and how you believe God is real. But it's not for me." I saw the disappointment on her face, and felt bad that I had been so blunt, but that's where I stood. It took very little time for the expression on her face to change, and then she went on as if she had never asked the question.

And that was how the next several months went with her. Except as time went on, I was the one telling the stories. Because things at home were escalating.

Kyle had started the "dry-drunk" symptoms again, and that kept me on edge pretty frequently. Toward the end of my second trimester, he had started disappearing again, and I was sharing my fears with Lonnie on a regular basis. She was always encouraging, and infrequently would add in our conversations, the possibility of "another way" for me. A place of peace and joy—things I knew little about. I kept my distance from the "salvation" conversation, but listened intently to her words of encouragement. I was always shocked when I would thank her for what she said, and she would smile and reply, "Not my words, Leslie. Those are Jesus' words." A feeling would come over me that I was completely unable to explain. It was distantly familiar, but I couldn't explain why. And I began to have difficulty fighting it.

The tension and stress I felt at home was in stark contrast to the feelings I had when working with Lonnie. Sometimes I felt like the old nursery rhyme about Humpty Dumpty. I had fallen off so many walls, so many times, I couldn't imagine who could possibly put me back together again. And my walls seemed to be getting taller and wider each time. I didn't understand what was happening to me, but I looked forward to going to work, even in those later months of my third trimester. I tried to keep her words in my head as I drove home each night. I tried to hang onto the feeling I had when I repeated them to myself. I did this frequently when Kyle was trying to push buttons so he could find an excuse to leave and drink.

My curiosity had started growing about this "Jesus" person she shared with me, the person I had only heard about in Sunday school as a young child, in a movie—*King of Kings*—as a 10-year-old, and for a few months in a youth group, when we lived in Columbus. This curiosity haunted me. I would get close to wanting to know more, but then would run away—as if I was afraid of something. But what? It reminded me of a starving animal who wants the bread you have for them, but is too afraid to get close to you. It steps a few feet closer, and then dashes away, stops, and looks back. Because it's still hungry. Hungry, but afraid of the giver of the bread. Can he be trusted? Will he hurt me? Is it worth the chance of getting close, so I can eat the bread?

Was I afraid, too? Afraid to trust? Afraid of getting hurt? Afraid to believe? I wasn't sure, but what I did know was I couldn't continue to live like I had been for all these years. I needed to make a better life for my kids, so maybe I needed to take a chance. A chance on Jesus . . .

Part Two

The Plethora of Miracles Begins

11

The Day I Met You . . .
My Shining Knight Appears

You may remember from *The Making of an Orphan*, I shared that I was waiting for my knight in shining armor to rescue me. I knew it wasn't Kyle, but I surely didn't know who to expect or when. Certainly not in a hospital room. In the midst of heavy labor. In a hospital gown. And no make-up. But this is where he showed up. And my life was forever changed.

Baby number two was about to be born. Actually, in all truth, it was baby number 4. As you know, I sacrificed two of my other babies. One for the convenience of finishing nursing school, because in my parents' home, at least in my father's opinion, education was more important than anything—even your grandchild's life. And the second sacrifice was my codependent need to please a second husband. To bow to someone else's demands. My life story.

I went into labor around noon on May 1, 1989. I called Kyle and left a message that I needed him to come home from work. We arrived at the hospital around 3 pm and I was admitted. The doctor said I was around 4 centimeters. They placed me on a Pitocin drip and Kyle's anxiety level increased to the point where I told him just to go out and get a cigarette and relax. He had picked up a 12 pack on the way to the hospital, so I knew he would be engaging in his typical ritual of "relaxing." Yes, you read that correctly. I had sacrificed a baby, so he wouldn't drink again—or leave me. And it was all in vain.

He only came up to the labor room one time after that first dismissal. He was pretty lit, and honestly, I was embarrassed to have him there, so my heart wasn't broken. But it was hard to be alone while going through contractions. A woman wants a hand to hold. Someone to do her breathing patterns with her to reduce the pain. Someone to just say, "I love you, and I am here for you. And with you. And I will never leave you." Someone like that . . . I had never known. And I still didn't.

The night had been long, and the contractions had been consistently increasing in pain, but they were not doing anything to my cervix. That was not the way it was supposed to be. I was supposed to be advancing in dilatation—at least a few centimeters with the degree of pain I was feeling. Because of the terrible experience I had with my first son, I was determined not to have another epidural. During that labor, they had over medicated me to the point that I could not feel my legs for almost 48 hours. I was unable to assist in the birth process because I literally could not feel a thing. No contractions, no urge to push. Nothing. So, they had to depend on the contraction monitor and my dilation to determine that I was ready to deliver. And then they had to use fundal pressure to deliver him successfully. It was a terrible situation and an awful memory.

So, I was determined when I got pregnant with this baby, I would not take a single medication—no epidural or pain meds. I was going to do it 100% naturally. The classes had been taken, and I had the breathing exercises down. And my son, Mike, had made sure I had a focal point to focus on during each contraction. He had given me his beloved Sarah—his stuffed triceratops from the movie, *The Land Before Time*— to be my point of in-depth focus as the contractions came and went. And it had been successfully working most of the 16 hours I had been here. But the doc had increased my oxytocin as much as possible to encourage the dilatation process, to no avail. The contractions were becoming unbearable, but physically, they were not doing the work on my cervix they were supposed to.

At around 5 am, the nurse came in to do her hourly check. I had felt a lot of pressure, so she helped me use the bed pan and then checked my cervix. As she was removing her glove, I saw her slowly shaking her head. I asked her how things were doing. She said I was still at 4 centimeters. This was really bad news because I felt the last contraction was the worst yet. She said she was concerned the doc would have to consider a forceps delivery or a possible c-section. Neither of those was a good option for me. She gave me some sips of water after checking my IV, and suggested I keep praying.

So, this praying thing was all unfamiliar news to me. Yes, as a young person, I had a nightly ritual of praying to God. I prayed for everyone to be safe. I prayed for my sins to be forgiven and any commandments I had broken to be forgiven. But it was not very personal. Not the way my friend described her prayers. The nurse who had been talking to me for months about a relationship with Jesus, and who had tried and failed to share her faith with me, suddenly came to the forefront of my mind. She didn't fail for lack of trying. I remembered all the times we had worked on the same floor—such an odd occurrence for two "float" nurses. I was reminded again how weird it was that *two* nurses would float to the same floor—on so many occasions. It was just beyond weird. But when I brought it to her attention, she didn't see it that way at all. *Even weirder.*

When she tried to talk to me about God or Jesus, I just put my hand up and said, "Thank you, but no thank you." She accepted it with so much patience, and just shared her "story" which was, coincidentally, so close to my own. We talked about our pregnancies and how much she and her husband looked forward to the birth of their baby. Something I just could not wrap my head around, because I never knew if my husband was happy or just counting the days till his next binge—and his ability to use the baby as his excuse to follow through.

As I contemplated the last several months of talking with this nurse, I remembered some of the things she had shared that had been almost like "miracles." Things that made no sense in the world I lived in—but to her were just "gifts from the Father's hand."

Father. There was a word to contemplate. What did it even mean? In my world? Not a heck of a lot. No trust. No love. No relationship. I had always longed for it with my dad. But it was never available. And this nurse believed, with all her heart, that God was a "father" who could supply all her needs. Really? A God I could not see, hear, or touch, but I was to believe He would do wonderful things for me? If my own father here on Earth would not do those things, how was I to believe a God in Heaven would do anything for me? It was the stuff of fairy tales.

Another contraction hit, overwhelming me. They were getting so much worse. Something had to give. I did not want a forceps delivery. Or a c-section. I held on tightly to the handles on the bed, purposed there for when the time came to push. Would I ever get to that point? My eyes were fixed on Sarah, my focal point. And as the pain began to decrease, and I saw the monitor needle dipping as it began its descent, I thought, "What if it isn't a fairy tale?"

As I took some deep breaths to relax, I silently did what I had done as a teenager. Only this time, I asked a few questions first. It sounded like this:

"God, if you are real, if you are the God my friend told me about, please do not let this delivery end up like my last one. Please let me go through a healthy delivery and let my baby be ok. I know I have been resistant to hearing anything about you, but I am reaching out now."

I immediately had another contraction, and I did what I wasn't supposed to do. I closed my eyes. This was supposed to make the contraction pain worse, and I learned quickly it was true. As it leveled out, I felt an odd warmth on my right hand. It couldn't possibly be my husband. He had pretty much stayed in the car the whole time, and I had not seen him since around 3 am. I thought maybe he had decided to join me, and slowly opened my eyes, hoping to see his hand on mine. But instead, I was shocked beyond belief.

I did see a hand. But a hand that was glowing—like fire. Bright, bright light. My breath caught in my throat as my eyes slowly traversed from the hand to the wrist to the forearm to the elbow to the upper arm and then to a figure standing there. Bright, like a blazing fire. I couldn't breathe, and immediately shut my eyes, recalling quickly that I had taken no drugs since I was admitted. And that in my past I had never done any psychedelics, like LSD, where I might be having a "flashback." And I had not taken anything before coming to the hospital. There was no logical reason I was experiencing what seemed like a hallucination. How could this be happening?

All those thought processes probably only took a couple of seconds, so I braved the idea of possibly seeing it again. With great anticipation, I opened my eyes, but the figure was gone. However, I could still feel the warmth where the hand had been. And something else was happening I had never felt before. Something that felt like warm water washing over my entire body, and with that sensation, a feeling I was totally unfamiliar with—peace. And a voice in my head saying, "Trust me." And just like that, I wasn't worried anymore about the birth, or the outcome. I shut my eyes again and bathed in it.

Suddenly, incredible pain gripped me. Another contraction was coming on strong. The monitor was revealing a big mound, and it was peaking when three nurses ran into the room. One of them yelled, "Get the doc up here! STAT!"

The contraction was still peaking and through gritted teeth, I choked out, "What's wrong? Is the baby okay?"

"His heart is decelerating, and you are crowning! We need to get him delivered!"

The nurse who had checked me earlier shouted, "That's impossible! I just checked her 5 minutes ago and she was 4 centimeters! She can't be crowning!"

The first nurse looked at her in disbelief. "Well, it may be impossible, but it's happening! Someone, get that doctor up here now!"

The contraction was subsiding, and I was able to finally begin comprehending what they were saying. None of it made any sense. Transition, the period between 7-10 centimeters is the most painful and most difficult time during the labor process. I keenly remembered Mike's birth. And the nurse said only 5 minutes had passed! Really? That experience I had—what seemed like a hallucination—was it? Or was it real? The words, "Trust me" played like a mantra in my head. It was all too much to comprehend. All I knew was I wanted my baby to be safe.

The doc rushed into the room at the same moment I felt a huge urge to push. He barely had his gloves on, when I heard him say, "He's coming really fast, try to push back on the perineum." And then I felt tremendous relief, and the doc was holding my baby boy. They cut the cord, wrapped him up, and handed him to me. The doc told me I had some serious 4th degree tears in my perineum, and it would take some time to suture me. The postpartum room was not ready for me, and they didn't have the bassinet warmed up or anything. They did get his weight and length, then handed him back to me. I didn't care about any of that. I was holding my baby boy, and he was nursing already. I experienced all the things I missed with Mike. It was amazing.

They explained to me that no rooms were available in postpartum for a while, and they would be placing me in a holding room, with my baby, until the room was ready. Then they would take him to clean him up. They rolled me into the room, and I just watched with incredible joy as my son nursed. The events of the last hour rolled in my head like a tornado. I couldn't grasp the possibility of it. The meaning of it. The incredulity of it. I knew, as a nurse, that what had just happened to me during the birth of my son was miraculous. I knew the experience I had prior to that last contraction was miraculous—it was not a hallucination. I knew the feeling that had washed over me was miraculous. What had just happened?

Almost an hour passed before they came to take me upstairs. I had that time to soak in all the mysteries of the day. I had yet to see my husband. I didn't even know if he knew I had the baby—or if he was even at the hospital. And I didn't care. Suddenly, my friend's face came to my mind. She and all the stories of "miracles" in her life that I had blown off as so much baloney. Well, they weren't baloney anymore. The possibility of them was very real now.

After I got settled in, washed up, and relaxed, I called her. I didn't know what to say. I didn't know how to begin my tale of miracles. She answered on the second ring, and I told her my son had been born. I told her all the expected details of weight and height, how beautiful he was, and all the other motherly details. Then there was a long pause as emotion washed over me. She asked me if I was ok. *Long pause.*

"Yes, I am more than okay. I know now, I want what you have. I want to meet Jesus."

12

Old Programs Out—
New Programs In

"Take your everyday, ordinary life—your sleeping, eating, going-to-work, and walking-around life—and place it before God as an offering. Embracing what God does for you is the best thing you can do for him. Don't become so well-adjusted to your culture that you fit into it without even thinking. Instead, fix your attention on God. You'll be changed from the inside out. Readily recognize what he wants from you, and quickly respond to it. Unlike the culture around you, always dragging you down to its level of immaturity, God brings the best out of you, develops well-formed maturity in you." Romans 12:2 The Message

I would love to tell you after that miraculous experience in the delivery room that I lived happily ever after. I have heard many stories of people's lives radically changing after a spiritual/salvation experience. And they experienced an immediate new life. That wasn't the case for me. There was a lot to undo. A lot of de-programming and re-programming had to take place. A lot of internal voices, and a few external voices, had to be quieted—no, eradicated. Jesus had His hands full.

Worse yet, I was completely oblivious to needing all those things to happen. *Come on! You should know it by heart now! Until someone tells you that you're messed up, you don't know it.* What I had been living all my adult life was just a continuation of all I had experienced in my childhood. Different players. Different locations. Different traumas. But it was the same old stuff.

However, one thing had changed. I had hope now. As I read through the One Year Bible my nurse friend had given me, it wasn't like reading Greek anymore. Things were making sense. I read about miracles and the love of Jesus, and the sacrifice He made for ME. That was often too much to take in. More than not, I felt He did that for other people, but not for me. How could a holy God forgive all I had done? How could *He* want a relationship with *me*? Those would be questions to haunt me for many years to come. But there was hope now . . . that He might. And there was a loving Jesus who knew how to begin the process.

A few months had passed since my baby was born, and my friend from work, who had witnessed to me and given me the Bible, invited me to her church. I had not really been to a church since I was a teenager, except for my wedding. I have to admit, her church made me nervous, and I felt awkward. I had that internal message that if anyone knew what I was really like they wouldn't want me there. It was also very different from the church I had attended. I was perplexed by why they danced around, spoke in languages I didn't understand, and were very loud as they worshipped. Kyle came with me a few times, but he felt even more awkward than I did because he had never been to a church at all, and he had not made a commitment to Jesus yet.

After a few months, I began to notice I was making excuses not to go to church on Sunday and that didn't feel right either. So, I finally went to the pastor, who was a very wise man. He told me he would rather see me go to another church than continue to feel uncomfortable here. He explained that if I felt that uneasy, I may drop out altogether, and that was not his goal. I felt so relieved by his kind words, but I had no idea where else I should go. So, I asked. He smiled at me and patted my hand. "God will guide you where He wants you to be."

Well, that was a little much for me to take in at the time. How would God possibly show me where I should go? How could He? I left our meeting with some apprehension, but decided to trust the pastor's words. Trust was a new concept for me. Like the words I had heard Jesus say in the labor room, "Trust me." But I agreed I would trust and see what happened next.

At the time, I was working 3 days a week at the hospital. When I checked my schedule for this week, each day I had been placed on a different floor. I was on the float team still, and it was a hassle to be moved around that much, plus it was not good for the continuity of care for my patients. I usually had more consistency in my schedule and made a note to myself to talk with the supervisor.

I knew many of the people I was working with on the first day—nurses as well as the unit secretary, but I had never talked about anything spiritual with any of them. So, I decided to take a chance and share my concerns about my church situation. The unit secretary quickly spoke up and said I should try her church because everyone was so nice. She gave me the name and I tucked it away.

The next day I worked, I was with a whole new group of people, and I thought I might get some different suggestions. So, I had the exact same conversation with them. One of the nurses spoke up and invited me to her church. She gave me the exact same name of the exact same church. Okay. This was weird.

So, on day three, and on another new floor, when I received the same response—but this time coming from a nurse AND a unit secretary—I just said, "Wow!" No mistaking it! God was telling me where HE wanted me.

Looking back, I now see His divine placement on those 3 floors. It was to purposely meet those people who would guide me to the church where my walk with Jesus would be nurtured and watered, and where I would find the family I never knew I needed. It was the first of so many miracles God would perform to entice me into His Kingdom. He knew I needed them because trust was an unrealized emotion for me—or maybe, more appropriately, something I had learned was non-existent in my world. He had a lot to teach me about trust, love, safety, security, family, and relationships. And He immediately began to place people in my path to guide me.

One of the first people I talked with and came to know quite well through her Sunday school class was Lynette. And boy, did God have a plan for her in my life. Well, that's a bit of an understatement. The reason I have a life today is because of the incredible investment she made in me and my kids. It was her godly counsel that woke me from my unhealthy slumber. This was the person who had the guts to tell me, "You need some help. I think you should talk with a counselor, a Christian counselor." And so began my journey to healing. And Lynette stayed by my side through all the painful, ugly mess I had to unravel.

So, Lynette became the person who told me something was wrong, that something was "off". She cared enough to open my eyes to what I could not see for myself. Many people may see something in someone—the way they act, or talk, or isolate—but are fearful of saying anything. Afraid of hurting feelings. Afraid of them getting angry. Afraid it may affect their relationship. BUT, what if you don't? What if you just let them spiral down—into who knows what else—and a word from you could have prevented it? I would have given anything if someone had told me years earlier I needed help. I knew from high school that my counselors felt I did, but my dad shot down all their efforts. And he shot down therapy in general. So, I had no frame of reference from which to choose what was good for me. I only knew what I had lived. My messed-up life was my "norm."

When Lynette opened that door for me, I kicked off the blanket of denial and dug in deep to find my way on the road to healing. And I did it while pregnant with my third son (I don't think I have ever done anything the easy way.) I unpacked a lot during that time. But not all. There would be much more down the road for me. The deeper stuff. The darker stuff. The stuff I would try to run from . . . even as a Christian.

God knew exactly how much I could handle while He was teaching me about Himself. Showing me His faithfulness. His sovereignty. His trustworthiness. If I had seen all of my past that I eventually needed to look at—all at once—I would have run from Him. I would not have appreciated all He still needed to reveal to me. I would have been like my dad. "If there is a God, why does He allow so many bad things to happen to good people?" I would never have become the person I am today. The person God created me to be.

Let me take a break here and share an example of that profound love He showers on us. When I started writing Forgiven Much *in 2004, it was after 7 years of me fighting against God's urging that I write my story. Following an accident at work, that left me unable to walk without surgery—a surgery that was delayed for over a year—I woke one morning and said, "What am I going to do now, God?" To which He quickly replied, "You will write the book." I finally gave in.*

I actually tried to write it as I have written The Making of an Orphan, *and this book, in the present day. I got through the first chapter, was very happy with it, and saved my work. The next day, I sat down to continue. It was gone. Nowhere to be found on the computer. Frustration. So, I wrote it again, trying to remember how I had constructed it before. I even added a second chapter. This time I was super careful about saving. The next day . . . gone! No frustration this time. Pure anger. Called a friend and she suggested getting a floppy disc and saving it that way. (Yes, this was a long time ago). So, I bought some floppy discs, and that night I sat down to begin again. I felt I had duplicated, as best I could, what I had written prior, saved it to the computer, and to the disc. Next day, put in the disc . . . nothing but hieroglyphics. What???*

I was done. I looked up at the ceiling and yelled, "I am trying to do what You told me! But this just keeps happening! Do You want me to write the book, or not?" I didn't ask it with any expectation of a reply. I was just venting my anger and frustration. But an answer came.

"Daughter, you have never once asked me how I want you to write the story. I don't want it to be in the modern day. I want it to be in Biblical times. I want you to give your life experiences to Mary Magdalene. I want the story to focus on my Son."

And so Forgiven Much *was born. But I did not understand until I wrote these last two books why He had me do it that way. First, He knew I would not do it halfway—that I would completely research the needed info to write about Mary Magdalene. And in that process, research the Bible and other resources for reference about Jesus. So, I did, and learned so much more about who He is.*

Information I would not have discovered had I written it in modern day. Truth I needed to comprehend, to be able to receive all He still had to show me.

And in the process . . . teaching me I could trust Him.

Secondly, He knew I wasn't ready to write my story because He knew I still had pieces to heal. Remember the story about Nick and the party? Yeah, I thought about how to include that in Forgiven Much, *and immediately dismissed it. Too much shame. Too much guilt. Too much darkness. No one could ever know that happened to me. It's what defined who I believed I was. I had never told a soul, and I wasn't starting now. There were many things I wrote about in that book that were already healed, and some were still a little raw, but He knew I could write about them—as someone else. As if those things were happening to another person, so I wasn't personalizing it. He knew I wasn't ready to write it—as myself.*

God only gives you as much as you can handle. There is a Scripture in 1 Corinthians 10:13 that says, "The temptations in your life are no different from what others experience. And God is faithful. He will not allow the temptation to be more than you can stand. When you are tempted, he will show you a way out so that you can endure."

There may be some who would argue my interpretation of this, but what it has meant to me—during critical times in my life—was that I was healing in stages, because God knew I could only handle so much at each level. He knew I would be tempted to run if it was all thrown at me at once. This will become important to know as I share the chapters in my life where he took me deeper. Into the dark places that shaped who I believed I was, not as He defined me. Those traumas that made me feel unworthy to even attend a church, much less believe a holy God could love a wretch like me. He knew . . . and He guided my healing process with a wise and gentle hand. A hand that only a loving Father possesses for His daughter . . . His princess.

13

A Miraculous Conception

"For with God nothing will be impossible." Luke 1:38 KJV

At the beginning of my healing journey, I went to a counseling group Lynette had recommended. I expressed my concerns about my marriage, and marriage counseling was recommended along with me attending a therapy group once a week. I was nervous about the group, and even more so when I discovered it was a group for women who had been sexually abused. *What?* I had not been abused as far as I knew. But I liked the women in the group and believed I would get something out of it. So, I faithfully went every week.

Kyle and I attended 4 marriage counseling sessions before he dropped out. It wasn't because the counselor wasn't doing his job, it was because he was. He wanted to meet with Kyle and dig deep into his family of origin and see what life had been like for him growing up. That lasted exactly 2 sessions. Kyle's family history was filled with trauma, rejection, and abandonment. And he wasn't going to deal with any of it. He told me he re-lived that stuff enough and he didn't need a reminder. At that point in my life, I was not educated to the fact that this is exactly what he needed to do—so he could finally let it go. But both of us were aboard the same ship of ignorance. The difference was, I was ready to jump overboard and dive into the dark depths of what that part of my life had done to me. He wasn't able to.

I pretty much knew this marriage was over, but was afraid to be a single mother with 2 kids, and so when Lynette had recommended the counseling, I believed it could possibly save our marriage. However, in the meantime, I was determined to do nothing that could further attach me to this man. Which included not getting pregnant again. Though the occasions were few and far between, we were super careful to have no accidents.

So, this is a lot of detail, but without it, there is no way you can see the miracle that took place. After Kyle stopped counseling, I saw things going downhill. He had started working with a new group of construction workers and he admitted they were all into "crack." Kyle had done a lot of things, but had not gone there yet. However, the changes in his behaviors put me on guard. So, following a pretty good week, when he was home and seemingly invested in me, we had an intimate moment. I was not terribly worried because I was having my monthly visit, AND I used a spermicidal sponge, AND he used a condom. Absolutely, no way was I going to take a chance. It was actually the last intimate moment we ever had.

Kyle disappeared several days after that. I didn't know where he was and no one else seemed to know either. When he finally came home, his whole paycheck was gone. And his second wedding ring was missing. One thing about Kyle is he told the truth, so when I asked about the money and his ring, he admitted he had used them to buy crack. I felt like someone had sucker punched me. I knew this was the end.

Three weeks later, I was cleaning up the living room and swooned. Ears ringing, lights flashing, I felt like I was going to pass out. This happened every time I conceived, but I knew that was impossible this time. So, when other symptoms showed up, I decided to see my OB/GYN. I shared the details of the encounter with my husband, and he assured me it was probably a false alarm. But it wasn't. The pregnancy test was positive, and the ultrasound proved I was so early, all he could see was a peanut with a heartbeat—5 weeks gestation. I couldn't believe it! I asked him how someone could possibly get pregnant during their period? Plus, all the protection? He was as perplexed as I was. I went home not knowing what would happen.

Those concerns were answered quickly because Kyle didn't want the responsibility of another child, and when payday rolled around again, he disappeared. This time he didn't come back. My friend, Linda, who I worked with at the hospital, said she had seen his car at a rinky- dink motel where you could rent a room by the week. She offered to drive me there. The anticipation of what I would find was overwhelming, and when I saw his parked car, I felt my heart flutter. I decided to knock on the door in front of where his car was parked, and when he opened it, a woman was in the bed behind him. I began to cry and asked him how he could do this knowing I was pregnant, and before he could say anything, the girl laughed and said, "Hey, I'm pregnant too!" He told her to shut up and tried to catch me as I ran back to Linda's car. I quickly got in and she drove away with him yelling for us to come back. There were only a few more times I saw Kyle after that, so the saga will continue . . .

Now, my past will tell you, after a breakup, I dove deep into drinking and partying to try and numb the pain I was feeling. And where I sit today, I can't honestly tell you that even my faith walk would have prevented it. Old habits die hard. But that couldn't happen this time, because I was pregnant. God knew exactly what I needed. He knew the pain I would feel from the present relationship ending, and he knew the pain I was going to feel from what was coming down the pike as I walked through my past with the counselor. And he knew how much I loved kids, and consequently would never do anything, ever again, that might harm them during my pregnancy.

The next eight months were going to be a hell I had never expected or remotely considered. But He knew. So, God brought a baby into my life. He wanted me to move forward on that long road to finding the person He created me to be. This pregnancy—this baby—became the catalyst God used to begin to heal His daughter. It was a miracle. And it was far from the last.

14

God's Arithmetic

"'Bring the whole tithe into the storehouse, that there may be food in my house.
Test me in this,' says the LORD Almighty, 'and see if I will not throw open the floodgates of
heaven and pour out so much blessing that there will not be room enough to store it.'"
Malachi 3:10 NIV

One of the toughest lessons for me to learn was about tithing. As a single mom I couldn't justify giving money to the church when I had so little for my family. I made decent money as a nurse, but after Kyle left, I had to take on all the financial responsibility in our new home, while being pregnant. And, well, it just didn't make sense. Lynette told me about the Scripture in Malachi and how God would bless me, but I had been raised by a father who pinched pennies better than Scrooge himself, so cognitively I was unable to work out that kind of math in my head.

However, this bothered me so much, even when I tried to sleep, I knew I had to do something about it. I sat for a long time and thought about how much money 10% would eliminate from my budget. It just made no sense that this was going to work. But I needed to start getting some sleep at night, so, I pulled out my finance book that Dad had taught me to make, and started re-doing it. I deducted the 10% first for the tithe, and then figured out the things in stone—like the mortgage, car insurance, etc. Adjustments needed to be made to the variables like food, entertainment, clothes, and other miscellaneous items in the budget. These took the biggest hit. $40 a week doesn't seem like a lot until you don't have it in the budget. Shaking my head, I decided I would try it for 3 months. I couldn't see how it was possibly going to work, but I committed for 90 days. Still shaking my head, I put the finance book away,

93

and said out loud, "OK, I am taking the challenge in Scripture. I know you can do miracles, but this one will be a big one for me!" *Little did I understand in those days how the Holy Spirit works on our hearts, even in the middle of the night, but oh my, I would learn. I would definitely learn.*

Three years earlier, I had gone to the dentist complaining about a tooth being sensitive, and after doing x-rays, he stated he saw no issue with it and then told me it was because of my bite. This was odd to me because I had always been told as a young person, I had a perfect bite, and would never need braces. He told me teeth shift sometimes. He fitted me with a mouth guard to sleep with each night, which eventually caused TMJ. It was very painful, and I could not even open my mouth to eat for several days, as if I had lockjaw. After a week of not wearing the mouth guard the TMJ symptoms subsided, and I didn't go back to that dentist.

The tooth I had complained about continued to hurt and was sensitive to cold and pressure. Since the dentist said it wasn't a cavity, I didn't know what to do. So, I ignored it. About a month later, I was eating some peanuts, and felt this incredible pain and then crunching where that tooth was. The tooth had fallen apart. I had teeth fragments in my mouth and when I rinsed my mouth, what remained of the tooth was throbbing. I called a new dentist's office and during that visit, he told me the tooth was badly decayed and that was why it had broken apart. I shared what the other dentist had told me, so the new dentist ordered my medical records. At my next appointment, he showed me the old X-rays and the cavity in the tooth. The other dentist had completely missed it. He then told me I would need a root canal.

Needless to say, I was pretty angry. So angry, I called a local attorney and asked if I had a case of negligence with this dentist. I sent him my information and records, and he said I had a case. He told me it wasn't going to be a big case, but it should earn me about $4000. Not great for all the pain and suffering I had already experienced, plus the two failed root canals, and the subsequent loss of the tooth I would experience in the future. But it would at least pay for the root canals, extraction, and dental bridge I would eventually need to get. Better than nothing.

Then the lawyer stopped communicating with me. I called on a regular basis, and he was never available, nor did he return my calls. I even tried visiting his office and he was either "out of the office" or "with a client" but never available. This went on for two years. I had just recently had that tooth extracted and insurance paid a large part of it, but the bridge I needed was going to be $1000 and as I thought about my new budget cuts to allow for tithing, I realized it probably wasn't going to happen. I had not tried contacting the attorney for a few months, but decided to call him again. This time I had the idea of using my middle and maiden names when I introduced myself. And he took the call.

"Hello, Ms. Taylor, may I help you?" Very cheery and friendly.

"Hi, this is actually Leslie, and I apologize for using my maiden name, but it seemed you would not answer my calls when I used my real name. It has been a long time since we talked. I have since had 2 root canals in an attempt to save the tooth, but I just recently had to have it extracted. What happened to my case?!"

There was a long silence. I actually thought he had hung up. Then, "I am so sorry. I dropped the ball. Things got busy and I put this on the back burner. I do feel terrible. However, too much time has passed now to bring the case. But I want to make it right. I promised you $4000 in compensation money. If you will allow me to give you $1000 per month over the next 4 months, I will pay you, out of my pocket, what I promised you would get."

I was completely speechless! I agreed immediately and thanked him. He took down my new address and said the first check would be in the mail this week. I hung up the phone in shock. This was a miracle. Then I remembered: I had only been paying my tithe for a month. My tithe was $40. At some point in church, I had heard about God blessing us a hundred-fold when we tithe. I wasn't exactly sure what that meant yet, but in this situation, it was a pretty easy math equation. That's exactly what I was getting: $4000! I couldn't believe it. God had done it!

But that isn't the end of the story.

Yes, I did continue paying my tithe—faithfully. I even paid a tithe on the $4000— without even thinking about it. I had seen a miracle. I didn't understand it, but I didn't have to. I used that money to get my dental bridge, and to pay off all of the doctor and credit card bills I had accumulated since Kyle left. By October, I was pinching pennies again, and I had had some pre-eclampsia symptoms with my pregnancy, so had missed some work, too. Things were definitely tight, but at least I didn't have the pressure of the bills I had been able to paid off. So, I had no regrets. But my baby was due in a month, and Christmas was coming. And there just wasn't any extra.

One night at work, I prayed with a patient, and a complaint was filed by the roommate. The person I prayed with had been my patient for over a year, as she came in regularly for treatment. She was now terminal and asked if I would pray with her to ask Jesus into her heart. I always wore a cross necklace, and over the time I had known her, she asked a lot about my faith. My testimony to God's power in my life and my faith in knowing my eternal promise of Heaven, caused her to want to be sure she could be confident of where she was going. I was glad to offer her that peace. She passed the next morning.

The following week I was called down to the director's office and asked about the situation. I was informed there are chaplains for that purpose; it was not my job to pray with patients. I explained that her time was not promised, and the chaplain was not always in the hospital, but my words fell on deaf ears. I was asked to promise not to do it again. I explained I could not do that. For her, that was not acceptable, and I was told if I could not promise, she would ask for my resignation. I explained my situation as a single mom, plus being pregnant, and I needed my job. She said I had 30 days to change my mind, or turn in my resignation. I told them I would think about it. I needed to work the rest of my schedule, and they let me.

I worked a double on Thanksgiving to make some extra money for Christmas. My boys spent the day with my parents. I hated missing the holiday with them, but this also guaranteed me having Christmas off. And I was trusting I really wouldn't lose my job.

The next day was Friday, and my baby was due any day. Looking out at the yard with all the leaves still there made me realize that chore needed to be done today, because after the baby was born, it wouldn't happen. So, I wrangled the boys and told them if we could accomplish this chore, I would take them for pizza and to see the new Disney movie, *Beauty and the Beast*. Both boys were all in, so we managed to fill 18 large leaf bags, after much hiding and jumping in the leaves.

After the pizza and the movie, we came home, took baths and got into our PJ's. The boys wanted to watch the Christmas movie, *It's a Wonderful Life*, before bedtime. No argument from me because it's my favorite and I was definitely worn out. I was even able to catch a few needed ZZ's during the movie. Then when I stood to turn the TV off, my water broke. Mike and David were so excited, and our pre-made plans went into action. Mike called our friend, Dru, who was going to keep them while I was in the hospital. David went and got his and Mike's overnight bags, and I got my suitcase. After Dru left with the boys, I called the hospital, and then Lynette picked me up. Eight hours later, I was holding my new son, Matthew.

The next day, while nursing my baby, I heard a bit of a ruckus outside my door. I put my son down in his cradle, and started for the door when Kyle came in. He was obviously drunk and tried to hug me. The nurse was outside the door and asked if I wanted her to call security. I nodded and then saw Kyle heading for the cradle. Before I could stop him, he picked up Matthew and hugged him. My heart felt like it was trip-hammering as I feared Kyle dropping him. Walking up to him, I tried to take the baby, and he just spun away from me and almost tripped over the bedside table. At that moment, two security guards came in and one held Kyle while the other took Matthew and handed him to me. He kept repeating in his slurred speech how much he loved me, and things would be different if I just gave him another chance. I had nothing to say. So many chances had been offered, and I was all chanced out. "Sorry, Kyle. That ship has sailed." The security guards led him out with little resistance, and he continued to say he loved me, even as he reached the hall, where he began to yell it. The tears were pouring out of me as I held Matthew. Not because I regretted my decision, but because I realized, at that moment, he truly wanted to be a different person, and was completely incapable of doing the hard work to get there. For the first time I saw him through Jesus' eyes, and it made me very sad for him. It also made my gratitude that much richer, for what God had already done in my life. I would only see Kyle once more.

The next day, I learned from Dru that both my boys had come down with chicken pox and the pediatrician said they would not be able to come home with me until they were past the communicable stage. So, I had three days with my new baby at home. That time was precious, but it also gave me way too much time to think about how empty the bank account was and how Christmas was only 3 weeks away. I had no idea what I was going to do to provide a good Christmas for them. I didn't even have any food for a decent Christmas dinner. There was a lot of worry. And a lot of tears.

I decided to call work and try to salvage my job, but I was told, without a promise to call the chaplain for anything spiritual in the future, I could not return to my position. I couldn't make that promise, so the supervisor referred me to the director. This probably wasn't going to be good. And it wasn't. My 30 days had passed, without an answer from me, and they had terminated me. Wow. My first thoughts went to the promise I had believed about tithing. Maybe it was only a one-shot deal. And I had had my one shot.

The boys finally came home, and I pretended the best I could to be happy. Someone had donated a tree for us, and I felt so blessed for that but also more saddened there was nothing to place under it. That Saturday, we spent the afternoon decorating our tree. Watching the excitement in their little faces as they anticipated Christmas morning was heartbreaking. The money I had made from working my double had to be used to pay the mortgage. That would be my last paycheck.

So, on Christmas Eve, I had to say something to them. We did our usual Christmas Eve tradition of reading the Christmas story in the gospel of Luke, then I read them *The Night Before Christmas,* and we sang Christmas songs. When I tucked them in that night, I said, "Guys, I know you're excited because Santa comes tonight. But I feel you need to understand, sometimes he doesn't come to every house. Sometimes, he runs out of gifts and can't make every house on his list."

David was silent, but Mike looked really sad and asked if they had not been "good enough" and was that a possible reason. I quickly assured him that wasn't the case, and then he said, "Well, I am going to pray and believe he will have enough toys in his sleigh to leave us something!" This brought immediate tears to my eyes, and I quickly hugged them both and kissed them goodnight.

I truly believe there is nothing harder than being a parent who can't provide for your kids. The shock of losing my job, and now having nothing for them for Christmas brought me to a very low place. I left their room with tears pouring out. I heard Matthew fussing and realized it was feeding time, and as I nursed him, I wept the whole time. *Why are you letting this happen, God? Have I done something wrong? Is this a punishment? I thought I was doing all the right things. I just don't understand.* These thoughts kept vacillating in my head, as the tears fell.

Gratefully, Matthew fell asleep quickly and as I was placing him in the bassinet, I heard a knock at the door. Who in the world was knocking on my door at 9 pm on Christmas Eve? I was grateful to still be dressed and quickly went to the sink and wiped my face. As I opened the door, the mystery was still dangling in my brain. It was a lady from my church, Mrs. Wood. And she had a huge grin on her face.

"Hi Leslie! We have a few things for you. Do you mind if we bring them in?" I looked into my driveway and a pickup truck was backing in. The back of it was filled with bags. Two men jumped out of the truck and collected some bags and began to bring them in. Another truck had pulled up in front of my neighbor's house and the two men from that truck also began to pick up bags and bring them in. It was all bags of food. And by the time they were done, it was a total of 40 bags! I could not believe my eyes, and I wasn't seeing much anyway because I was crying so hard. I hugged Mrs. Wood and thanked her. She was about 8 inches shorter than me but a little ball of fire, and she looked up at me and said, "Oh, honey! We aren't done yet!"

The four men had gone out to their respective trucks and the one parked at my neighbor's was now backing in where the first truck had been. And this truck was full of wrapped Christmas gifts. And I mean full! By the time they had unloaded everything under our tree, you couldn't walk in my living room. There were no words to say. My heart was bursting. I hugged all of them as they were leaving and through a flood of tears thanked them for all they had done. As Mrs. Wood was getting ready to leave, she gave a big smile, and with much authority said, "Don't ever forget how much Jesus loves you!"

Jesus. Yes, this was His birthday we were celebrating and just look at what He had done for us. A hundred-fold? This was a thousand-fold!! I quickly checked on all the kids and all were soundly sleeping. I silently praised God for that. It took me over an hour to put all the food away. Included was absolutely everything we needed for our Christmas dinner. It was a miracle.

Back in the living room, I had to move furniture around so in the morning the boys could get to the tree. I could not believe how many gifts there were. I had just told my two sons that Santa might not come . . . and now this.

The next morning, I was miraculously awake before the boys. I got my camera, picked up Matthew and finished nursing him as I stared at the tree. I was still in awe. I was also amazed at how long the boys were sleeping, when I heard Mike shout, "Wake up, David! It's Christmas morning!" In seconds they were in the living room. Both had their mouths wide open! Mike, in his theatrical way, slapped his forehead in disbelief, and said, "Santa not only came; he left his whole sleigh full of toys!" Then, quite dramatically, fell straight backwards.

It took over an hour for them to open all their gifts, and they helped me open mine and Matthew's as well. It was a morning none of us will ever forget. I could not stop thanking God. He kept proving to me over and over again, He was faithful. And He was true to His word. I felt so undeserving of all the love He lavished on me. So, when a mother and daughter showed up at my house that afternoon with two more boxes full of gifts, I was beside myself. They said they adopted a family to bless every Christmas, and this year they had chosen us. Most of these gifts were for me and they were all so special. I didn't know how to thank them enough, and the daughter explained she had been a single mom. She understood. I was overwhelmed.

There are so many more examples, but not enough pages in this book to tell them all. *Yes, when John shares in his gospel how Jesus did so many things, that if they were all written down, the whole world could not contain the books that would be written, I understand exactly what he meant!* But there is one more example I want to share of His incredible grace and love.

I eventually got another job, but not before I got behind in my bills. My dad had helped me with my mortgage in February, but March was ticking away. Dad and Mom had come to visit one afternoon, and while they were there, a friend from church stopped by. During our conversation, she asked how I was doing financially, and I explained things had been tough, but God had been blessing me. I then said, "He even helped me get my mortgage paid last month!" We both praised God for that, but not everyone was happy to hear what I said.

Dad immediately retorted. "God didn't pay your mortgage, I did."

I was a little taken aback, and responded, "Dad, I meant God led you to do that." But he didn't like that either.

"God didn't lead me to do anything. I did it to help you. All on my own."

Well, it made for an awkward moment, and it wasn't the last. My parents were babysitting one afternoon while I went to a doctor's appointment, and since I was approaching 30 days past due for March, I braved the moment and asked Dad if he could help me one more time. I explained my first paycheck was coming during the first week of April, and I would pay him back half in April and half in May. He was reading the newspaper, and peeked over the top of it and with a sardonic smile, he quipped, "Let God provide it for you. I won't be." And that was the end of that.

The next day was March 31, and if I went over 30 days, it wouldn't be good. I went to bed that night and prayed profusely for an answer. All I could do was hope. I had no work the next day, and caught up on some house chores, then remembered to check the mail. As I sat at the kitchen table going through it, I saw a letter from the IRS. Oh, no! I couldn't take any more bills, or bad news. I was unaware of any mistakes with my taxes the prior year, or any other. I was afraid to open it.

Inside was a letter explaining there had been a mistake with my taxes from two years prior and I was given a refund. When I opened the rest of the letter, I stopped in midair as I saw the amount. It was one dollar shy of my mortgage amount! I was incredulous. I immediately got in the car and deposited the check in my bank account and then called the mortgage company. Even though there had been a fee for it being late, they were waiving it because of my circumstances, so I had exactly enough to cover my mortgage.

Wow, God. Just wow.

15

Putting Things Back Where They Belong

"Flee from sexual immorality. All other sins a person commits are outside the body, but whoever sins sexually, sins against their own body." 1 Corinthians 6:18 NIV

One of the first Christian retreats I attended as a new believer was a District Singles retreat at River Valley Ranch. I was excited because they had horses, and we had an opportunity to ride. A handful of people were attending from my church; two of them were good friends of mine. I was nervous because I didn't know what to expect, or what was expected of me. My divorce from Kyle was fresh and the idea of meeting someone was exciting. It was a 3-hour trip, and the ride was a lot of fun, as I got to know more about the people with me. *Please keep in mind, during this time, I was still in the beginning of my healing process, so my codependent thinking, and behaviors were still racing on.*

When we arrived, I got my room assignment, and was so relieved to be with my two friends. One of them, Linda, I had worked with at the hospital. The other was my friend Denise, we had been introduced through Lynette, and had become fast friends. As we unpacked and made up our beds, we found ourselves comparing notes on the guys we had seen who were attending. It was like being a teenager again.

The schedule was pretty easy. Friday and Saturday night was dinner followed by a session with the pastor. Saturday and Sunday morning was breakfast, followed by a morning session with him, then lunch. Suzy, the person in charge of the District Singles, told us at dinner Friday night that this pastor was young but really powerful at bringing awesome messages. Denise, Linda, and I were in complete agreement with her after attending the session that followed.

He talked candidly about purity and abstinence until marriage. He even explained that those of us who had been married could claim "second virginity" as we waited for a new spouse. That sparked my interest, and I wanted to better understand what he meant. He shared how we could ask God to make things "like new" as we turned our lives over to Jesus, because He "makes all things new." He wasn't implying a physical change, but a mental and emotional change—especially if we had been in a marriage where betrayal or infidelity had taken place. Well, that was about every relationship I had ever been involved in, so I was all in. The pastor was young, and his name was Matthew. As he described the love and devotion he had for his wife and family, I began weeping. This was the type of relationship I had always longed for— and now prayed for—and he even shared she had been a single mom, so it left me feeling there was some hope for me.

That night, us girls talked into the wee hours about how awesome Pastor Matthew was and how we wished we could clone him! We conceded that there must be guys like him somewhere and maybe there were even some here this weekend. It was a sweet thought to end our day on.

The next day we barely made it to breakfast on time. All of us were scrambling to share the single hall bathroom for showers and make-up. We discovered quickly we were not the only women there who thought the pastor was pretty special—he was the main discussion at breakfast. Our next session was as informative as the first as he shared the story of the woman at the well. Jesus called her out on her life, but did it with love and grace. Most of the accounts in the Bible were still unknown to me, and this guy made the stories come to life. As he talked, I thought about my own life and wondered how it would look in ten years. I felt strongly I needed to have a man in my life at all times and— little did I know—this was one of the symptoms of my codependency. I needed to always have someone in my life to concentrate on helping to fix. This kept me busy so I never had to look at my own issues. I had so much to learn.

Pastor Matthew ended the session with a prayer and as the group moved out of the room, Denise and I talked about going to visit the horses. Linda was quick to be included. We were nearly the last in line as the room emptied, and as we approached the door, I heard my name. "Leslie, could you hang back a few minutes?" It was the pastor. I didn't even know he knew my name. I did an automatic eyebrow arch as I looked at my two friends and relayed I would join them soon. Linda gave a mischievous grin, and I whispered, "He is too young for me!" Denise laughed and they both grinned as they left.

Now let's take a quick break and look at this. I had admired this man for how he talked with so much admiration and love for his wife and how loyal he was to his family. Why would I even joke about, or even entertain the thought, he might be keeping me because he "found me special"? Here is another symptom of codependency coupled with my constant need for affirmation. Anyone who paid attention to me was a possible relationship—now or in the future. This is a classic outcome from the neglect I felt as a child. The conversation that was about to take place was one of my first awakenings to how unhealthy I was. And it became a driving force for me to change.

"Leslie, I was wondering if I could talk with you for a few minutes?" His eyes and his voice were gentle but focused and, as I began to sit, he directed me to the door that opened to the gym. There were several people there playing volleyball and with the noise, I was confused why he wanted to talk in there instead of this quieter location. "To honor my wife, I never meet with a woman alone. I always am sure other people are present."

Well, this was Greek to me. I was learning so much from this man about what marriage and relationships were supposed to look like. Certainly nothing I had ever been taught. As we sat on the bleachers, I felt more and more self-conscious, especially with the thoughts I had earlier. And those feelings were about to multiply exponentially.

"Leslie," he spoke so gently, I could barely hear him. "I feel God has given me a message for you, and one He wants me to share with you. It's not an easy message to hear, but one I feel will change your life."

Well, now I was ready to run. I didn't need this on what was supposed to be a vacation for me. Could I not ever escape the voice of condemnation even at a church retreat? But his eyes and his gentleness kept me captive. I didn't know this man but for whatever reason, I felt I could trust him not to hurt me—at least not intentionally. I dug my fingernails into the edge of the bleacher and waited.

"Leslie, I feel you are a woman who has known many men. Like the woman at the well, you have been looking for love in all the wrong places. Love is not about sex. And sex does not have to be about love. But it was God's plan that the two are inseparable—in the bond of marriage—nowhere else. But the culture we live in has watered down His plan and sex has become casual and without commitment—and often without the emotional bond of love that is so necessary, especially for the woman. God's plan was that a man and woman come together after marriage and become one—in body, in spirit, and in their soul. Outside of marriage, this is only true for the body. You still come together and become one, but without the holy commitment of the marriage covenant. God's plan for us does not change just because we choose not to obey Him. Are you with me on this?"

I felt so strange as I listened to him explain this, but so curious as well. "Yes, I am with you. I am trying to understand."

He smiled at me and continued, "So, when you come together with a man, and then go your separate ways, he takes a little bit of you with him, and leaves a little bit of him with you. Spiritually, this can be dangerous because you could have pieces left with you by someone that may not be a good person. And you have given away parts of yourself that you need to be the whole person God created you to be. So, why am I having this conversation with you? Because last night, as I prepared for the message today, God put you on my heart so heavily, I couldn't shake it. He told me I must have this conversation with you today. The Scripture He gave me was 1 Corinthians 6:18. It says, 'Flee from sexual immorality. All other sins a person commits are outside the body, but whoever sins sexually, sins against their own body.' In our culture today, sex outside of marriage is not considered a sin, but in God's eyes it is. You shared last night that you are a new Christian and did not grow up in a Christian home. I doubt you were taught this, but God wants you to know it now. He has a plan and purpose for your life that is bigger than you can imagine. And He wants you to be free."

I was in shock and didn't know what to say. This was absolutely not what I had been taught by my dad. My mom had always told me I needed to be a virgin until I married, and I made it to the age of 18, but then the voices of all my friends confirmed how old-fashioned this was. Now I am hearing it is a sin, and one that affects my whole body! How do you undo that? "Pastor, this is a lot to understand, and I feel strongly that what you say is true, but I don't know how to go backwards. How do I undo what has already been done?"

He grinned. "I am glad you asked. We are going to pray for God to supernaturally remove all the parts that have been left behind, and we are going to ask Him to return all the parts taken away. He wants things to be put back where they belong. I have some oil, and I will anoint you and we will pray that right now."

That would not be a problem! I actually felt like the woman at the well must have felt. The excitement that had overwhelmed me at my salvation experience was just like this. New life. New me. How much more did God have for me? I wasn't sure, but was very excited to find out.

My heart felt like a trip-hammer. Excitement and fear co-mingled at such a level, I was breathless. I leaned my head toward him and shut my eyes. I felt him form a cross on my forehead with the oil, and he prayed the prayer. He then asked God to give me a heart to accept a sense of second virginity and to honor it until I married again. He then asked for blessings over me and my family. Then he said "Amen."

I don't know how to put into words how I felt, but I literally felt different! Lighter. Feelings I can't put into readable language. I felt new! I was weeping uncontrollably and thanked him over and over. He, too, was tearful, and said, "This is your new life. Go and walk in it."

I couldn't wait to tell Denise and Linda. I was so excited. The way I felt reminded me of the story, *A Christmas Carol*. When Scrooge wakes up after his third visitation and realizes he is still alive, he dances around his room saying he feels like a baby. That was me. I wanted to dance! I wanted to tell the world! Gratitude was oozing out of me so fast I didn't know how to control it—vacillating between laughter and tears. I thanked the pastor again and wanted to hug him, but felt it wouldn't be appropriate. So, I asked first, and we hugged, and then he told me to go share what God had done for me.

16

Do You Want to be Healed?

"When Jesus saw him lying there and learned that he had been in this condition for a long time, he asked him, 'Do you want to get well?'
'Sir,' the invalid replied, 'I have no one to help me into the pool when the water is stirred. While I am trying to get in, someone else goes down ahead of me.'
Then Jesus said to him, 'Get up! Pick up your mat and walk.'" John 5:6-8 NIV

Almost a year had passed since the retreat at River Valley Ranch. My desire to heal had been amplified after my experience with Pastor Matthew, and I had been studying a lot about codependency in an awesome book by Frank Minirith and Paul Meier called *Love is a Choice*. As I read it, I repeatedly said to myself, "they wrote this book about me." It was life changing to see how all of my issues from childhood had led me to become the person I was—with the skewed thinking I had. It helped me realize those things I had internalized and blamed myself for were not my fault and how I had been a victim of much abuse—emotionally and physically. There was a lot to grieve. And a lot of re-programming needed to take place.

But my counselors felt there was much more underneath the surface of the codependency. Some of it was touched on in that book, but I was in a lot of denial. Especially about my dad. Recently, I had been journaling about memories from my young life that were so fragmented, I was not even sure what memory went where. I had "snapshots" of things I had experienced, but no order, or understanding of how they fit into my past.

During this time, I was working as a behavioral health nurse and doing psychoeducational support groups for women dealing with childhood sexual abuse. The girl who was co-facilitating with me had found a 2-day conference on sexual abuse, and our supervisor approved it for us to attend. The timing was uncanny. It was called, *Counseling Victims of Sexual Abuse: The Three Stages of Healing*. One of the concepts she taught us was how people, who have dissociated from some childhood trauma, often have floating memories—like my snapshots. She showed us her teaching model—a large brick wall—with bricks missing in the wall, but above it were several "floating" bricks. She explained that the wall represented our lives, and the floating bricks represented our lost memories. She taught us that, through counseling, the client is often able to recall those memories and fit the bricks back into the empty slots.

This intrigued me, and I wondered if this model could work for me. After returning home, I shared this with the two ladies who had formerly been my counselors, but with whom I now co- facilitated groups. They agreed, since in my journaling it seemed I was recalling more and more snapshots, that it could be possible my brain was trying to put some order to them. They encouraged me to keep journaling. Over the next several weeks, I wrote a lot about each of the "snapshots" I had in my head. This is what I remembered:

- My mom always bought me white chocolate, even on holidays—never milk or dark chocolate—because she said I didn't like it. I didn't remember ever saying that.
- Several years earlier, my husband and I had taken our oldest boy to Hershey Park, and we did a tour of the chocolate factory. At the end of the tour, we rode an escalator down to the first level, and on the way down were pictures of their candy bars and how the wrappers had transitioned over the years. I was holding Mike in my arms and showing him the pics and when I got to the 1950's picture of the candy bar, I instantaneously felt like I couldn't breathe. My heart started pounding and I practically threw Mike into my husband's arms, ran the rest of the way down the escalator, and began hunting for a bathroom. I had never had a panic attack, but as an RN, knew what they were, and realized I was having one. But why?
- A very specific floor plan of a house, but unaware where it was or when we lived there.
- Standing behind my mom while she threw dishes at my dad as he ran out a door – and he was in his Navy uniform.
- A compulsion, I had never understood, to spread my legs during intimate times with my husband. Almost like a "show me" behavior of a curious young child. It was disturbing to me, but something I seemed to have little control of.
- A life-long sense that my mother was always jealous of the relationship between me and my dad.

A few weeks passed, and I felt strongly I needed to ask my parents about the floorplan in my memory. I had sketched it several times, and took my best drawing with me to their house. Mom was not home, so I asked Dad if he could help with it. After I showed it to him, I got the weirdest reaction.

"Why do you want to know about this floor plan? Why are you asking?" *Odd*

"I am working on some things with my counselor, and she has asked me to write what my memories are. I can't remember where this is, so I thought you guys would."

"Have you said anything to your mother about this?" *Wow, super odd.*

"No, Dad! What's the big deal? Where is it?"

"It's our house in Hawaii. Why are you, all of a sudden, wanting to bring up things from the past?" *Now I am feeling suspicious about his attitude.*

"Dad, I am just trying to get well. I am working on myself and trying to understand why I do the things I do. I have been in two bad marriages, and I need to know why I pick people who are unhealthy and end up hurting me. Why are you acting like this?"

"I just don't want you bringing up stuff to Mom that is going to upset her or cause trouble!" *He seemed angry and anxious—simultaneously.*

"Why would asking about a floor plan cause trouble, Dad? What happened there?"

"Nothing, Karin! Just drop it. You got your answer. Just don't talk to your mom about it!!!" *Now he was furious, and walked away in a huff.*

I just stared at him as he stomped into the kitchen, poured himself a bourbon, and then went out onto the porch. Never looked back. He was dismissing me. Something I was very familiar with anytime a subject involving feelings or emotions was brought up. I stood there a few more minutes, wondering if I should wait for Mom to come home, or just leave. I decided to leave. The drive home was quicker than usual—not because of time, but because I don't think I was aware of anything around me as I drove. What just happened?

I got home a few minutes before the boys were getting off the bus, and it was Friday, so that meant "camp-out night." I started campouts with my boys soon after Kyle had left us. It was a fun night of starting a fire in the fireplace, ordering pizza, or cooking hot dogs in the fire and finally, s'mores and a movie! It was a blast, and the boys loved it!

It was that time of year when the kids brought home candy bars to sell for a fund raiser at school. Mike was very excited to bring home his box of almond/chocolate bars that day with the hopes of selling some around the neighborhood, and possibly at church on Sunday. I told him I would help him by walking with him to the neighbors the next day, and also letting people know on Sunday.

It was May, and the next morning we woke up to a super gorgeous day! Spring had begun to show itself in full. The boys had baseball in the morning, and afterward, as always, I picked up Happy Meals for them on the way home. As they ate lunch, Mike reminded me about the candy, and remembering David had already tried to sneak a bar, I knew it was a good thing to try and get them sold. I reminded David how much candy he had eaten for his birthday the week before, and if there were any bars left, he could do a chore to earn the money to buy one from Mike. Though disgruntled, he agreed. When we got home, I made them change out of their baseball uniforms, and commenced to walk the neighborhood circle.

Apparently, a lot of other people were enjoying this beautiful day, because we only found about 7 people who were home, but all were looking to consume a chocolate bar! Out of 25 in his box, we only sold 9, and Mike was not happy. I reminded him there was still tomorrow at church. Both services were usually well attended, so he was content with that. That evening we had our traditional Saturday night dinner, whichever one we didn't do on campout night. So, this time it was pizza. The boys went and collected kindling for the fire while I ordered the pizza. Saturday was *Dr. Quinn—Medicine Woman*, followed by *Touched by an Angel*. We started our fire, ate dinner in the family room while watching the shows and, as always, made s'mores.

After stories, songs and prayers, I tucked the boys in, and stood an extra few minutes at their bedroom doors. This is what I had always longed for growing up. Just to know my parents were nearby, and that they loved me. Traditions. Consistency. Faith. Hope. Just time spent with me. Those weren't things my parents understood—or even knew about. I felt blessed at that moment to be able to give these things to my boys. But I felt like there was something nagging at me . . .

I went back to the kitchen and gave Thunder the dinner leftovers, as always. Thunder was our new member of the family. Lynette had heard about a dog that had been found on the docks in Salisbury, and told me her maid had him at her house. When I met him, it was love at first sight. He was huge! When he stood on his hind legs, he could look directly in my face, and I am a tall girl. The boys loved having a dog, especially one they could practically ride like a pony. He would lie in front of the TV, and they would use him like a giant pillow. It blessed my heart to see how quickly this dog had become part of our family. His loyalty reminded me a lot of Reeshie.

Thunder waited patiently for me to get done with the boys, knowing his reward was coming. He followed me into the family room, where I stoked the fire, gave him his dog biscuits, turned on the TV, and sat back to relax. The first ad that came on was for Hershey's chocolate bars. Wow, it looked really good! Hmmm. I couldn't remember ever having eaten one. And I had a box of them in the kitchen. There was no discussion. No argument. No hesitation. I went and got the box, brought it back into the family room, reclined in my chair and began to eat one. And then I ate another one. And another. And another. Until the box was empty.

I had no idea what I had been watching on TV. I had no memory of going through the whole box of bars. When I realized there were no more in the box, I literally gasped, as if discovering it for the first time. Whatever just happened was beyond my comprehension and seeming control. I suddenly realized I was beginning to feel very sick. Within minutes, I was in the bathroom and $16 worth of candy bars was being flushed down the toilet, along with my son's hopes for big sales at church. So many emotions were swirling in my head. Shame. Embarrassment. Guilt. Humiliation. And more than anything else . . . confusion. Utter and complete confusion. And fear. What just happened. And what was I going to tell Mike?

I let Thunder out one last time, turned off the lights, locked up and headed to bed. After doing all my nighttime routine, I took some Pepto Bismol—just in case—then laid down to do my evening devotions and Bible reading. I had been using a One Year Bible ever since becoming a Christian, and tonight's New Testament reading was in John, chapter 5. I had read the story of the man at the Pool of Bethesda, many times. Tonight however, certain words seemed to float up off the page—as if highlighted for me to pay special attention to them. Words used to describe those at the pool: BLIND, LAME, PARALYZED. Then the description of the man Jesus was focused on. "One who was there had been an invalid for 38 years." I wasn't sure what all this meant but I felt the Holy Spirit lead me to read it again . . . and then again. I remember thinking how codependent and victim-sounding this scenario was.

Jesus' question, "Do you want to be healed?"

The man's reply, "Sir, I have no one to help me into the pool when the water is stirred. While I am trying to get in, someone else goes down ahead of me."

Jesus had not asked him that. He had asked if he wanted to be healed, but the man was unable to do anything but continue to offer excuses. He was a victim. The ability to feel hope, or experience rescue from his situation, was not even a consideration. Only excuses.

I laughed out loud as I thought about the excuses I had made in my life to do what I knew I shouldn't do or not do what I knew I should. Like what had just happened with the candy bars. What I would say to Mike, or what had driven me to eat something I had never liked in my whole life was still a mystery. The person I had become wouldn't do something so destructive to her body. It was just not me. Something so compulsive. So crazy. No, I had little room to judge this man Jesus was speaking to.

Then I noticed what I had NOT noticed as I had read and reread this passage. The man had been an invalid for 38 years. Wow! Snap! I was 38 years old. There had to be a message here. Along with the words blind, lame and paralyzed. And no sooner did I think that thought,

than I heard the voice in my head I had come to know at the birth of my second son. It was Jesus. "Karin, do YOU want to be healed?"

I immediately began to cry, and all the journaling I had been doing, combined with the words of my counselor, came flooding to the forefront of my thoughts. I did not want to go there. I recalled my reaction when my counselor had asked me, "Have you ever thought that your dad may have something to do with your abuse?"

I felt rage rip into me. "NO way! He is my hero!" I had already shared many of the things with her that I didn't recognize as abuse—completely denied them, with ferocious denial—even after she explained they were abuse. Now, things were vacillating. Those questions, plus the way my dad responded to my inquiry about the floor plan. Plus, my out-of-control binge tonight. Plus, the journaling I had been doing . . . Well, abruptly, they all seemed like things I had to look at. But I didn't want to. Like the man at the pool, I had too many excuses. I closed my Bible, turned off the light and tried to forget it all. As I laid there, I realized Jesus had addressed me as "Karin." I knew that wasn't an accident either. I needed to sleep. Sleep and forget.

***

The next morning was the typical Sunday rush to get everyone dressed and fed for church. I had laid out all the boys' clothes, awakened them, let Thunder outside, and then proceeded to get breakfast underway. It was here I finally contemplated what I would tell Mike. There just wasn't anything that sounded reasonable—especially that his mother had binge eaten all of his candy in a dissociative state. As I was getting the last bowl of cereal poured, Mike came into the kitchen asking where the box of chocolates was. He knew he had left it on the kitchen table and was peering around the kitchen. I stalled by telling him to sit down and start eating his cereal, but that fell on deaf ears. This was important—and he needed me to understand that.

I swallowed hard, asked God for His forgiveness in advance, and proceeded to lie, straight-faced, to my son. "Sweetheart, I am so sorry! Last night I decided to eat one of your bars while I was watching TV, and I left the box on the floor. When I got up this morning, I found that Thunder had gotten into it, and ate the whole box. I am so sorry."

Mike exploded. "Mom, how could you have done that? What am I going to do about the money I owe for them?"

I hugged him and silently asked for forgiveness again. "It's okay, I will give you the money to cover the cost of the bars, and I will ask your teacher to give us another box to sell. I know you enjoy doing that so much. Again, I am so sorry."

He seemed to be assuaged for the time being, and I could finally take a deep breath. At that moment, I decided to add a visit to the altar on my to-do list for Sunday. I hated lying to my son, but had no idea how to explain something to him I myself was clueless about. I decided to definitely call my counselor the next day and work through this.

We had a great day at church, followed by our monthly meal in the gym. This was one of my favorite events because of the tremendous feeling of family. It was what I had always wanted while growing up—a big family with meals together, picnics, games—anything and everything that exemplified belongingness. I hoped it was something my kids would treasure as much as I did.

I rarely drove back home on family Sundays because we would have to turn around in such a short time and come right back for evening service. So, I kept the boys there and we would either play some basketball in the gym or play ball on the field. Sometimes, I even let them take turns sitting in my lap and drive the van around the field. They loved that!

I liked Sunday night service almost as much as Sunday morning service. It was testimony night and one of the things that had really grounded me as a believer were those early days of listening to people share all that God had done in their lives. The blessings and the miracles they had experienced. So many times, I listened and thought, "If God can do that for them, He can do it for me!" The stories were many of the "aha" moments in my early walk with Jesus.

This particular night, the kids were in class downstairs, and I was sitting behind a man who I had previously heard share how much Jesus had done in his life. He had been into drugs and alcohol, and I could relate so closely to his story of childhood trauma, and his attempts to numb his pain. This night, he stood and began to share a new story of how God had used him to help another man who was dealing with addiction. As I listened, instead of the uplifting and encouraging feelings I usually experienced, I was feeling horrific guilt and shame. It was all over me. Suddenly, I did not want to be here anymore. I didn't want to hear any more.

No, the truth was, I didn't feel I deserved to be here. This was a place for good people— not someone like me. My heart was racing, and I felt I had to get outside to get my breath. I realized I was crying and darted out of the pew and into the foyer. I sat on the bench, barely able to breathe. I was holding my head in my hands and asking myself over and over, "What is wrong with me?"

I heard the sanctuary door open, looked up, and saw Lynette standing there. I couldn't even look at her. She sat next to me and asked what was going on. I wanted to explode. In anger. In fear. In confusion. I didn't know how many emotions one person could experience all at once, but it was happening to me. I moved away from her on the bench.

"Don't touch me, Lynette. I have no business in this church. I have done so many bad things in my life. I don't know what I was thinking that it was okay to come here."

"Les, what's going on? You have asked God to forgive you. You have told me all your stuff and it's under Christ's blood. You have been forgiven."

I felt like my lungs were on fire. "No, you don't know everything! If you did, you would not be my friend! No one in this church would! I have no business being here. I will just wait till the service is over and get the kids and get out of here."

Lynette's smile was genuine, but her voice was firm. "You will not leave until you promise me you will call your counselor and talk with her when you get home. I think God is getting you ready to recall something painful. Maybe the things you have been journaling about, and all this guilt and shame you are feeling, are related somehow."

I immediately felt myself calming down. My heart wasn't racing anymore, and I could take a decent breath. But the tears were coming in torrents now. She started to rub my back, and I looked at her with tears pouring out. "I don't know what's going on, but I have to get past it. This weekend has been a nightmare."

Lynette was gentle. "That is often the case. Just remember the Scripture, 'Weeping may last through the night, but joy comes with the morning.' Trust that God will walk you through all this."

We hugged. What would I do without this lady? At that moment the kids all came running down the hall from their class, and Mike asked me if I had told Lynette about Thunder eating his candy. I swallowed a guilty lump, looked at Lynette and whispered, "Tell you later."

Sleep indeed came easily that night. After I called my counselor, and set an appointment with her to come to my house the next day, I tucked the boys in, and called it a day. I felt like my head was swimming, but asked God, out loud, for relief, and a quick and happy end to all of the weekend's events. As soon as I lay down, I was out.

***

Jackie came over after I got David and Matthew down for their nap. Mike was still in school, and the house was quiet. I told her every gory detail of the past weekend, and expressed my complete and utter bewilderment at the events that had taken place. She smiled and almost duplicated what Lynette had said, "It sounds like a memory is about to be revealed to you."

First, she wanted to hear about the journaling I had done regarding the "snapshots," so I pulled out my journal and shared with her what I had written, which actually was little more than an in-depth description of each memory. She then told me she wanted me to lie down somewhere that would be relaxing and comfortable. I suggested the recliner in our family room.

After I lay back in the recliner, Jackie prayed a beautiful prayer of peace and protection over me, and asked the Holy Spirit to come and reveal what it is He wants me to know. Her voice was so soft, and I felt my body relaxing. After she finished, she asked me how I was feeling, and I told her I felt very relaxed. She asked me to close my eyes and then said, "I want you to go back to the place in one of your snapshots where you are standing behind your mom, and she is throwing dishes at your dad. Can you see that?"

"Yes. I can see that."

"Now. I want you to tell me, Leslie. Are you wearing any clothes?"

I looked down at my body, and at that moment, I had been transported back to our house in Hawaii. I was 3 years old, standing behind my mom . . . and I was naked. My mom was screaming at my dad. He was calling her crazy as he was grabbing his uniform hat. He threw open the front door as the dishes were flying all around him, and he barely made it out without getting hit, as the plates crashed into the walls and door. I was scared, but behind me, I heard this beautiful, soft, and familiar voice.

"Come here, let me cover you." It was Jesus. He was sitting in a chair behind me. He reached for me and wrapped me with a cloak he had on his shoulders. He pulled me close to him and I realized I was shaking. Not from seeing Jesus, but from what I had just witnessed between my parents. I buried my face in his neck . . . and I could smell Him. It was a sweet, beautiful aroma I had never experienced before. He held me for the longest time, and I suddenly realized it was quiet, and just the two of us were there.

After a few minutes, he told me he needed to show me something. I clung to Him tighter and kept my face in his neck so I could keep smelling that wonderful aroma. I could even smell his hair. Then He said again, "I need you to let me show you something."

I began to shake again, and whispered, "I am too scared."

"It's okay, I am going to be with you. In fact, I am going to be holding you just like this, and I won't let go. Trust me."

There it was! I knew I had heard that voice before, but didn't know how or when. But that one statement, "trust me" was so familiar to me. I clung tighter to Him as He stood up and walked through the kitchen toward the bedrooms. I knew this floor plan well, and I knew where He was taking me. And He stopped where I expected He would—at my bedroom door. It was shut and as He reached for the doorknob I clung even tighter. "Please don't make me look! Please!"

He hugged me gently but firmly. I felt so protected. And that was not a terribly familiar feeling for me. But it was so wanted, and so desired. And right now—so needed. "It's going to be okay. I am right here, and I will not leave you."

Jesus opened the door and waited for me to look. I was stubborn; almost defiant. This was more than I could bear. He kissed my cheek and again repeated, "Trust me."

I slowly turned in His arms, and saw myself on the bed, naked and laughing. My dad was also laughing and tickling me. Every time he tickled me, I threw my legs wide open in ecstatic joy. Whenever he gave me a bath, we played our "tickle game." When mom was out shopping. I began to chuckle in Jesus' arms at how much fun I could see myself having!

My dad was dressed in his Navy uniform, and I noticed on the bedside table was a candy bar. A Hershey's chocolate bar to be exact. It caught my breath when I noticed it, but I didn't know why. Dad was laughing with me and said, "One more time!" He held his arm way up in the air and slowly came down to tickle me again, and the anticipation caused me to laugh even harder and spread my legs even wider.

Then Dad reached for the candy bar and said, "Here you go! That was fun!" As I saw myself take the candy, I felt someone pass by Jesus and me. It was Mom! She started screaming at Dad, "What kind of man are you? Get away from my daughter. What are you doing?"

Dad was scrambling and telling her it was just a tickle game. He said, "I just gave her a bath and we were playing a game." I was wondering why Mom was so angry. After all, it was just our "tickle game." But she wasn't just mad. She was out of control. She started hitting him as he ran out of the room, knocking over the grocery bags Mom had just brought home. He grabbed his hat off the counter and that's when the dishes started flying. He seemed afraid but at the same time, calm, as he told mom she was crazy, that she was making a big deal out of an innocent game. I saw myself hiding behind her and I felt the fear I had felt earlier . . . and then we were gone.

Suddenly, Jesus and I were sitting by a beautiful river with animals everywhere. Friendly animals. Rabbits and squirrels, donkeys and dogs, all kinds of animals just walking up to me to pet them. Jesus was sitting next to me, and I said, "But Jesus, there are no horses!" and instantly, two beautiful sorrels walked up from the riverbank and nuzzled me. This place was amazing!

Jesus had His arm around me, looking down at me. "I want to take you into the river, bathe you, and baptize you. And I have a beautiful white robe to place on you." He was smiling so gently, but inside I felt afraid. Baths were not necessarily safe places, and I didn't want to do it.

As if He read my thoughts, He hugged me tightly and said, "It's just a bath. Nothing more, and then I will baptize you. Come with me." I did, and He literally just dipped me in the water, and handed me a cloth to wash myself, and then he poured water over my head and wrapped me in the most beautiful white robe. It smelled like Him! Then we sat again by the river with the animals. I realized I was not a child anymore, but my actual adult age. He hugged me again and told me He had to leave now, but the things He had shown me were for my healing, and he told me to treat my kids as He had treated me. As He talked I realized He was beginning to ascend into the sky. I held on tight and begged Him not to leave. He smiled and continued to rise. "I will never leave you or forsake you. I am with you forever, right here." I saw Him touch the left side of His chest. And then He was gone.

And I was back in my recliner.

I looked around the room and Jackie asked me if I was ok. I asked her how much time had passed, and she said only about 10 minutes. She asked me what happened, and I began to weep. I didn't want to be back here. I wanted to be back at the river with Jesus. The reality of those moments I wanted to hang onto forever.

I told Jackie everything and she pointed out to me how every single one of the "snapshots" had been addressed in my "vision." I asked her if that's really what it was because it seemed too real to be just a vision. She explained that if I ever was to share it, "vision" was the best term to use, but she knew, as I did, what I had just experienced was much more than a vision.

***

In her book, *Light for the Journey through Dry Bone Valley,* my sweet friend, Patricia Boyce, wrote, "When we are hurt as children, those wounds impact how we think, behave, and relate to others, even after we become adults. The inner child absorbs and holds on to negative emotions triggered by caregivers who were supposed to keep us safe . . . Those terrified inner children don't disappear. The adults who harbor them have unknowingly found ways to suppress that fear."

This is how I had lived most of my adult life . . . and I had just been set free.

I have looked back on this experience, and have shared it numerous times. It was the beginning of my deepest healing from so many childhood wounds. It was the place where I literally watched a little 3-year-old girl, who had been severely traumatized, grow up in the arms of her protector. Her rescuer. Her Jesus.

It never loses its incredulity . . . and I never lose my awe . . . at a Savior who goes to the extreme of asking a terribly saddened woman, suffering in lost memories, "Do you want to be healed?" He knew I had been running from it my whole life. So instead, He chooses to help the little girl—living inside that adult body—face those painful memories in His arms. Within His safety and care.

No, this was not a vision. This was a miracle.

Part Three

Finding Truth Without Fear

From death to life
From darkness to a shine
From fear to a peace
I can't explain
From doubts to a hope
Holding on and letting go
Of all the empty promises of shame

From orphan to Your child
From a stone to running wild
From a seed in the ground
To breaking out
From a mess to a mess
A blessing to a blessing
A sea of failures bearing testimony

Love stretched out
On a tree screaming out
So that I could say
You've not forsaken me

You're the first and the last
My future and my past
Who I was
And who I will forever be
You are the in between

I was one way
But now I'm different
There was a clear change in
A Holy collision
Who I was
And who I'll forever be
And You are the in between.

"The In Between" by Matt Maher

17

Eyes Wide Shut

My experience with Jesus caused me to dig deep into God's Word and to begin on a road of self- improvement that would honor Him—professionally, emotionally, and physically. I already had a desire to share His awesomeness with others as my most longed-for goal. I had continued to work as a nurse, but knew my heart's passion had moved into the psychiatric realm. Jackie and the other counselor I had worked with had felt I had a gift of insight and wisdom in this field and encouraged me to nurture it. When they talked with their director, he agreed to have me come on board. So, I was supervised by him for the next year and began co-facilitating groups with Jackie. This led me to work in this field exclusively. When Jackie branched out and started her own counseling office, she hired me to work with her. And I began to take classes to become a certified psychiatric nurse.

Their appraisal of my work in this field was confirmation of what I had been told in nursing school when studying my Psychiatric Nursing curriculum. Those I worked with during my clinical psych rotation—my instructors and those at the hospital where we did the clinical work—had shared the same things with me. In fact, after graduation, I applied for a psych nurse position, and out of over 60 applicants at The Psychiatric Institute of Montgomery County, I was offered the position. The only reason I turned it down was because of a conversation I had with one of my med-surg instructors. When I shared with her the offer, she said I needed to get my med-surg skills down—in other words—accomplish them through practice. And that would not happen if I went the psych route. She felt if I ever wanted to change specialties, I would be "behind the 8 ball" in my clinical practice. This was one time in my life, I believe I should have followed my own beliefs and not someone else's. Clearly this field was my heart's cry.

Over time, I had begun to feel some loneliness for the first time since my divorce and at the suggestion of my friend, Lynette, I started inviting friends to my house for dinner and games on Saturday nights. We would often do Bible studies, too. Through this versatile group, I realized there was a need in many churches for singles who desired a place to hang out that was safe and uplifting. So, with another friend, I started a singles group called *Singles in Action*. We grew from around 10 regulars getting together for meals on Saturday night, to over 100 coming from the tri-state area, 3 times a month. As it grew, we had to move it to our church, to accommodate the numbers. We also did a lot of community work. From hosting dinners for the homeless on Easter, to visiting kids dressed as a favorite cartoon character on the pediatric unit of our local hospital during the holidays. We also did lawn and housework for the elderly, and helped out a lot of the single moms who needed work done in their homes. We had volunteers who offered "mechanic days" for single moms so they could get their oil changed and a tune-up—free of charge. We had weekend retreats twice a year with large turnouts at each event. It was a blessing to see the ministry grow.

I also decided to buy a stationary bike for my home. I began a workout plan when I was employed at the hospital, and had used their cardiac rehab equipment. My favorite piece was the Airdyne bike and so I saved and purchased one. Within a few months I was riding 10 miles in 30 minutes. I was feeling very confident as I continued to lose weight, and I could see myself getting stronger, both physically and emotionally. This new life with Christ had been nothing short of a miracle. I felt I had found a caring family for the first time in my life. I witnessed my kids growing up in Him as well. I loved the fellowship and was there any time the doors were open. And it was good.

But I had also begun to feel like something was missing. The boys continuously asked when Jesus was going to give them a new daddy. At their baseball and soccer games, they saw their friends being supported by their dads. They saw fathers playing with their kids whenever I took them to the park or when we went camping. They were quick to tell me how glad they were I was always present, but it just wasn't like having a dad. I understood those sentiments because I never saw my dad at any of my events.

It had been almost 3 years since my divorce and the boys asked if we could pray for a new daddy. So, we began to pray every night that God would bring someone into our lives. Someone to fill the missing spot. One night they prayed for a man like Samson. *I shuddered.* "Uhm, let's pray for a man like Joseph? Or Joshua?" They laughed and said they wanted a strong daddy. I didn't argue. A few months passed, and our prayers continued. *In retrospect, I wish I had taught them strength comes in many forms. Explaining to them physical strength may not be the most important. Strength of character. Strength of integrity. Strength of faith. Spiritual strength. These far outweigh physical strength. And looking back, I wish someone had made me aware of those truths as well.*

The life of a single mom has little time for rest. My days were usually packed, with a typical day looking like this: riding my bike for 10 miles, taking my shower, getting the boys dressed for school or daycare, breakfast, then onto work. After work, pick them up, start dinner, take baths, eat, do homework, play time, prayers, songs, and bed. There is seldom a dull moment with 3 boys and rarely a lack of fun or folly. So, one evening when I was making dinner and Mike complained the toilet had stopped up, I wasn't surprised. He was right. It was beyond the typical plunging or LIQUID-PLUMR fixes. A plumbing visit was never in the budget, but I had no choice. So, I made the appointment.

The plumber showed up the next day, and after snaking into the toilets, he discovered that the boys had apparently thrown some pencils in each one of them, and that was the source of the problem. He brought the guilty offenders to the kitchen and showed them to me—there had been 3 pencils in each toilet. I thanked him and continued to cook our dinner. I had taken no interest in him whatsoever . . . until that moment. I looked up and there was almost an immediate attraction. It was strange. Almost electric. I thanked him and asked if he wanted a burrito. He declined and I thanked him again for coming and fixing our problem. As he was leaving, he told me his name and gave me the bill, explaining the guy who was supposed to have come was busy, and that's why he had been called in. Interesting information I had not asked for.

After finishing my nighttime routine, I was sitting and doing my evening devotions, but could not get him off my mind. I asked God if this was the guy we had been praying for. I laughed out loud. He was kind of built like a Samson. The kids would love that! I did my nightly journaling, and asked God to open the door if this was the one. He had my phone number, so the ball was in his court. After a week, I heard nothing, and decided to call the plumbing company, to see if I could leave a message of thanks to him. *So, what happened to waiting for God to open the door???*

That evening he called. He asked me if I would consider going out to dinner with him. I agreed. The boys were thrilled that mom had a date, and when he came to the door, it was Mike who noticed how big he was. "Looks like a Samson, Mom. Maybe this will be the one we prayed for?"

I hugged him. "We will see, baby." I told my date I would be right out and then informed the babysitter I would be home early. I walked out to the car with him. It was a nice car, Pontiac Firebird. He didn't open the door for me. After I let myself in, and my door would not shut on the first try, I opened it again and tried to pull harder on the arm rest to shut it.

"Don't do that. The armrest is broken." His voice was impatient, as if I was supposed to know that. A thought flashed through my head, "Get out!" and say, "This date is over, dude. And don't come back." But I stopped and thought maybe I had read it wrong and decided to see how the rest of the night would go. He took me to a local sports bar and asked me what I would like to drink. I explained I didn't drink, so he ordered a drink for himself and a tea for me. We talked about a lot of things and for some reason I didn't share anything about my faith. That was odd for me, and I didn't even realize it until I got home that night.

The boys were very excited to hear what I thought about my date and I repeatedly shared, "Time will tell." After tucking them in, I started my devotional time with a prayer about this man. The incident about the door kept coming to mind. His reaction. The gut feeling I had when it happened. The temporary feeling of not being safe. I dismissed all these things with the argument that the rest of the night he had been so charming. Complimentary. *Charismatic.* I chose to shut down what seemed to be an answer to my prayer and give him the benefit of the doubt. Well, that is, if he called me back. Because I had decided I would not call him again.

A few days later there was a major winter storm. Schools were closed. My office was closed. The snow was coming down hard, and the boys and I were so excited! We loved the snow, and they immediately asked if we could make snow men and snow cream. I was all in!

As I was getting them dressed, there was a knock at the door. It was him. He had his work truck and wanted to know if I needed anything from the store. Since I owned a Volkswagen camper van, and they had very poor traction in snow, this was a blessing. I realized I did not have all the ingredients for the snow cream and, with the boys being so excited, I decided I would make a list and let him pick up what I needed. As I thanked him, I gave him my list.

When he returned, he not only brought the snow cream ingredients but also a few pizzas. I had no choice but to invite him in. We all ate together, and then the boys began asking to go out in the snow to play. He immediately agreed to go out with them. We had a great snowball fight and then built a few snowmen. I grabbed a large bowl and collected some clean snow, and invited him to join us for snow cream. The whole day was going so smoothly, it almost seemed like it had been planned supernaturally. He stayed all day, and after I got the kids to bed, he stayed longer. We talked about a lot of things including how much he loved kids, and especially how much he had enjoyed playing with my boys. You know, the kind of information that makes a mother's heart swoon. When he left, he asked if he could kiss me goodnight. I told him I couldn't because it would affect my ability to stay objective. So, he kissed me on the cheek and left.

I felt so confused. Once more, I sat in my devotional time and prayed, begging for an answer that he may be the one. Instead of an answer, I saw a clear picture of me telling him I couldn't kiss him and him kissing me on the cheek anyway. Every time I asked for an answer, I got "scenes" of something that had been negative—a violation of a boundary. The one in the car was a lack of respect, and this was also. And as I was pondering this, another scene floated to the surface of me letting myself in the car, instead of him opening the door for me. Another show of little respect. Again today, I had no desire to share my faith with him. And, again, I didn't understand it.

The next day was Saturday, and he called and asked if he could come over. It was December 4th, and I was planning to get the Christmas décor down from the attic. He said he would love to help me. My heart skipped a beat with excitement. This must surely be a sign that he could be the one. God knew how important Christmas was to me and the boys. And He was showing me we would not celebrate alone this year. This would be a great Christmas.

The boys were so excited he was coming over and asked if they could play in the snow with him again. This made my heart sing. I decided right there, this must be the answer I had prayed for each night, and those negative "scenes" I was having were from the enemy. That had to be the answer. Satan surely didn't want to see me happy, so he would use whatever means necessary, to ruin what God was putting into motion. And this was surely something God was orchestrating!

Or was it . . .

18

When Your Gut Speaks—Listen

"Rescue me from the grip of bad men and women, so I can live life your way." The Message
"Ransom me from the oppression of evil people; then I can obey your commandments." NLT
"Redeem me from the oppression of men, that I may obey your precepts." NIV
Psalm 119:134

Never ignore your gut. God made us with an innate warning system that begins in the pit of your stomach as the first alarm to danger. Ignoring it could lead to terrible consequences. This chapter is dedicated to mine . . .

This chapter is going to be a little different. Instead of telling you my story "as it happens," I am going to explain a few things to help you understand how the next part of my story came to pass. In my book *The Making of an Orphan*, I alluded to an unhealed situation that led to a later choice I made that was more devastating than any so far. Here is what I wrote:

I did a pretty good job at all of this—for a time. But, as I said before, there was one thing in my life I was so ashamed of, and with which I carried so much guilt, I didn't share it—even with my counselor. So, this left me with unhealed places, which left me open to making another devastating choice. You see, as long as I had no man in my life, I could keep it at bay. But it was there. Waiting for the right moment to raise its ugly head once again. Waiting for the triggers to ignite all the pain afresh. A wound, only superficially healed with a temporary covering that could easily be ripped off to expose the corroded infection below. It had kept me captive— unbeknownst to me. And this new choice was going to bring even more trauma. A choice that would lead both me and my kids down an ugly road. And consequently, it would inject them into this curse of generational trauma. The one thing I had tried so hard to prevent.

In Chapter 4 of this book, "The Whispering Voice" holds the story behind that unhealed situation. What happened to me in that chapter was identity-changing, life-defining, and the most self-depreciatory moment in my life. And *the voice* made sure I bought into every single negative word I heard about myself. Or who had anything derogatory to say about me. It made me doubt any good attribute I might have thought I had, and to accept any abuse coming my way as deserved—because I was such an awful person.

As long as I was single—and that incident stayed at bay—I could soak in all the healing Jesus had walked me through. I could stand on this foundation of sand that continually caused me to ignore that one life-changing event. The event which was so horrible I had never shared it with a living soul. Please don't think I am saying all of the healing that had already taken place was anything but genuine. I dealt with most of my issues: sexual abuse, codependence, relational issues, and also my parents' abuse, rejection, and abandonment. I had taken many classes on all of these, read multiple books, and felt confident helping others walk through these areas in their own lives. But there was something I didn't know. When there is an unhealed place, and that place is a core trauma, my susceptibility to fall back into a hole I thought had been filled was a real possibility. I had never dealt with trauma bonds yet—I had never even heard of them. And, boy, did I have them. Quite a few of them.

As, I shared earlier, God's plan to prepare me for the work He knew I needed to do was by encouraging me to write a book about my life. I fought it for 7 years but finally gave in and wrote *Forgiven Much*. I was led to write it as a novel with the protagonist being Mary Magdalene. I considered including this traumatic event in that book, but quickly countered, "No way!" Not even in a book that was fiction—where I had the ability to use author's license to entertain my imagination—was I going to take the chance that someone might think this event had actually happened to me. But, regardless, that book was His guidance into deeper healing, and writing it had regurgitated a lot of things in my life. I was a blank chalkboard waiting for the lessons to begin. And these lessons would be much more painful than anything in the past. Because the house of healing I had constructed on some undisclosed, shaky ground was truly built on sand, and I had not been transparent with anyone about it, not even Jesus. So, I could easily fall again. And I did.

The Scripture from Psalm 119 which I shared above was the verse God gave me as He was pulling me out of the miry clay I had fallen back into. And the drifting sand my house had been built on. And the muck that surrounded my feelings of worthlessness, that even His love had not dispelled. Because I wouldn't let them go. He helped reveal to me through those wise words of David, that when we are in a situation that is oppressive—when we are with someone who is oppressive—we can't see God anymore. We can't hear Him.

We can't obey His precepts, His commandments, or live life His way. The oppression blinds our eyes and deafens our ears. And for me—all I heard was *the voice*. But now it was coming from the mouth of the man I had married. The man with whom I had a precious daughter. The man I had trusted to care for myself and my children. The man I had trusted to provide for us. The man I had trusted to protect us. The man I had trusted to love us. And none of that was happening. Only oppression. I had married a narcissist, and I never saw it coming. I was blind-sided. And that blindness all went back to the superficially healed traumatic wound I had hidden so efficiently.

So, I ignored the "scenes" I was shown in the beginning of this relationship, directly after my prayers. I ignored the lies I discovered. I ignored that he came from a religious cult that went back for generations in his family. I ignored his claim that he had said a prayer for Jesus to come into his heart, but absolutely no one was there to witness it or testify to its authenticity. I ignored that he disappeared a few weeks before the wedding, leaving just a note that he couldn't marry me because his family would never speak to him again—then coming back and begging for a second chance but refusing to postpone the wedding. I ignored all the lies and deceit that were revealed to me in those 5 months before I said, "I do." I ignored it all. And I continued to believe in my heart that all these warning signs were just plans of the devil to keep us apart.

The next several years of my life were a living hell. This dark secret I thought I had hidden so effectively, was actually revealing itself as something growing larger and larger in my psyche, exactly like a tsunami will form in the ocean. The unseen earthquake on the ocean floor (the big T trauma) causes an enormous wave (trauma responses) on the ocean's surface. When the Earth's tectonic plates move and become displaced against each other (perception vs. reality), energy builds up (fight, flight, freeze, or fawn) and displaces the sea-floor plus zillions of gallons of water above it, creating a tsunami that races away from the center and builds into a deadly wave (anxiety, panic attacks, dissociation) when it reaches land. Things I thought I would never put up with again were happening.

- oppressive, controlling behavior
- adultery through pornography and affairs
- theft through mismanagement of my boys' college funds
- maxing out my credit cards because he had none
- abuse verbally, emotionally, and physically
- living in a state of poverty most of the time because he would not work
- . . . and this is the short list

And I was allowing them . . . but why?

I found out the answer one morning, after waking up, realizing the house was empty, and cried out, "Jesus, I am worse now than when I first met you. What is wrong with me?"

First, let me set the stage for that question. Ten years into our marriage, I had discovered he was having an affair. I caught them red-handed. And, unfortunately, 3 of my kids were with me. Another affair and another divorce were situations I knew I could never handle again. And I had made a promise to God on my wedding day. I made a covenant with Him. I had to make this marriage work. But it takes two for that to happen. This led to 2 years of me exhausting every avenue I knew. It also led to ever-increasing symptoms of betrayal trauma because he was not invested. As I shared in The Making of an Orphan, *the stages of betrayal trauma as addressed in Sheri Keffer's book,* Intimate Deception, *will lead you to many places you don't intend to go.*

My kids and I had prayed for a daddy and husband to bless us, not to make our lives worse than they had ever been. Why would God allow that? I shook my fist at God and said I was done. No more church. No more prayers. I was done. And I started drinking again. Every day. I was going to show God I didn't need Him anymore. I was finished. And I rebelled. I rebelled against God.

I had been on this 2-month rebellious road when I got a wake-up call. One night I was tucking in Matthew and leaning over to kiss him goodnight. "I love you, son. Sleep tight. Don't let the bedbugs bite."

"Mom, have you been drinking?" His innocent, sweet face made me want to cry.

"Yes, son. Things are pretty rough right now, and I just needed something to help me relax." That sounded pretty reasonable. I hoped he would think so.

His little face was sad, but intentional. "Mom, you always told us if we had problems, or if things were rough, we were supposed to pray and talk to God."

Well, out of the mouth of babes. Looking at his tender face, the tears started. "You are right, baby. That is what I taught you. And I promise I will from now on." And I meant it.

So, the next morning, I posed the question. "Jesus, I am worse now than when I first met you. What Is wrong with me?" And this is what He said, "If you are done with your two-month temper tantrum, I will show you some things." And for the next several minutes I felt like I was watching a video of all the times he had tried to stop me from marrying this man. All those initial, first scenes when I prayed for an answer. And the many other things like the difficulty in getting our marriage license, the loss of my driver's license so we had to postpone, the promises made before his disappearance, and the lies about why he left and quit his job. All of it. And I had viewed all of those— perceived all of those—as if they were ways Satan was trying to keep us from marrying. Wow! God had just reframed how very hard He had tried to protect me.

That evening, I went back to church. First time in a while. It was a Wednesday night and a friend I had not seen in a long time came to me and started sharing her wonderful experience with a new counselor she was seeing. When I asked who, she shared her name. It was someone I knew well, and I tucked away the information. I prayed that night and asked God if this was His provision, and I felt a resounding "YES!" was in my heart. So, I called to be sure there would be no conflict of interest, and set up my first appointment.

Over the next several months I shared all my woes of the last 11 years. She put me in a fabulous book called, *The Betrayal Bond*, by Patrick Carnes. Wow! I had not read a book that changed my life so much since *Love is a Choice*. Then one day I came to my appointment and was in for a shock. "Les, I can't help you anymore. I am sorry."

"What? Why?"

"Because you aren't being honest with me."

"That's not true! I have told you everything. I have kept nothing back!" *I felt incensed. Angry. Defensive.*

"Do you remember the color poster I asked you to do? Remember the bottom left corner of the picture was all dark and secretive? You told me you didn't know what it represented. You said you believed it might be something your dad had done but you had dissociated."

"Yes. That's exactly what I thought it meant." *But I was pretty certain my resolve was breaking wide open in front of her.*

"Les, I think you know exactly what it is. I think you have kept it inside for a very long time."

The tears were flowing freely now. Of course, I knew what it was. But how could I share with this person, whom I respected so much, something so terrible about myself? I was sobbing now, and she took my hands. "Just let it come." And so, I did. I shared every ugly and dirty detail you read about in "The Whispering Voice." Sobbing so hard I had a hitch in my breathing . . . and my voice. She reached for some tissues and when my crying had come down to a manageable level, she took my hands again.

"Leslie, what happened to you was not an orgy. What happened to you was a gang rape."

"Oh! That's not true! I drank the liquor! I took the pill! It was 100% my fault!"

"Les, that is what the devil would like you to believe, but tell me what happened when you woke up?"

"I screamed for them to stop. I begged them to stop."

"Les, look me in the eyes. Does that sound like someone who is participating?"

My breath caught in my throat. My head was spinning. She had completely reframed that night for me. This had happened to me over 30 years ago and it was now feeling like it happened yesterday. All the feelings were flooding back. I remembered the utter disgust I felt when I woke up; as woozy as I was, I was repulsed and embarrassed. She was right! I had been out cold when all of it was going on. And when I woke up, I screamed for them to stop. What she was telling me is what I would tell any of my clients if they had a similar story. That awful night, I had listened to *the voice*. And it seemed I had not stopped listening ever since that night. And it had caused me to allow all the abusive treatment I had accepted. I reached over and hugged her.

"Leslie, do you remember the day I asked you, 'What is it about YOU that allows him to treat you the way he does?' Well, now you know. You had internalized that event and defined yourself worthy of abusive treatment. And all the healing you had already done, you also dismissed as unworthy of you. Consequently, you allowed the abuse—both emotionally and physically. Now what are you going to do with it?"

"I am going to go home and sleep for a while before the kids get there because I feel like I have been pulled through a keyhole."

She chuckled, and then with more seriousness. "Les, you can expect the same physical, mental, and emotional reaction you had after the memory you had about your dad. For a few days you will feel a bit out of it. Lethargic. Fatigue. Your brain needs time to heal—it has kept that trauma shut down for a while. Be kind to yourself and take it easy." She reached over and hugged me, and I tearfully thanked her again.

The drive home was like being in a cloud. In fact, the rest of the day was. I had a couple hours before the kids came home, and I was true to my word by taking a 90-minute nap. Even upon awakening, I felt lightheaded, like in a surrealistic dream. But I was wide awake. I thanked Jesus for being my advocate, my friend, my healer, and my Savior.

Suddenly, it occurred to me . . . When I was happy and praying—feeling grateful for something and wanting to praise—it was Jesus I talked to. But when I was angry and felt I had been wronged or life wasn't fair, it was God I addressed. There was something to this, but I couldn't quite make the connection. And my head was in no shape to try. I picked up my Bible and looked at the reading for today in the Old Testament from the book of 1 Kings. The story of Naboth, Jezebel and Ahab. I knew it well and would read it tonight.

At that moment the kids began to come home. I put down my Bible, but felt strangely certain something else was on the horizon.

19

A Lesson from Ahab

"Then another message from the LORD came to Elijah:
"Do you see how Ahab has humbled himself before me?
Because he has done this, I will not do what I promised during his lifetime."
1 Kings 21:28-29 NLT

That evening with the kids was the best I could remember in years. They even saw the difference in me. I couldn't explain it, so I didn't try. When they asked where Dad was, I told them honestly, I didn't know—but there was no angst attached to it. No anxiety. No worry. Coming home late from work was a subject I didn't broach, and suddenly, I didn't care. Something had truly changed, and it felt good. Things still had a surrealistic appearance, but I knew it would pass as it had before. Life was good right now and I was wallowing in it.

We did our nightly routine of dinner, dishes, stories, baths, songs, and prayers. It felt like it used to be when I had been single and happier. I knew at that moment I could do it again. Yes, I was older. Yes, I now had 4 children, but I could do it with Jesus' help. It was a moment of complete clarity and surrender. And it felt good. It was the first time I had felt like this in close to 12 years.

After tucking everyone in, I went back to my room and got ready for bed. I was fully aware how easily sleep would come to me tonight. Picking up my Bible, I turned to today's Scripture in the Old Testament. 1 Kings 21:1-29. The chapter begins with King Ahab wanting to buy Naboth's vineyard. Naboth is a neighbor and is unwilling to sell his land as it has been an inheritance for generations. This causes Ahab to sulk, so his wife Jezebel decides to help. She sets up a contrived situation that makes it seem that Naboth has been disrespectful to the King, and is subsequently stoned to death. Here is the rest of the story as told in the Bible:

When Jezebel heard the news, she said to Ahab, "You know the vineyard Naboth wouldn't sell you? Well, you can have it now! He's dead!" So, Ahab immediately went down to the vineyard of Naboth to claim it.

But the LORD said to Elijah, "Go down to meet King Ahab of Israel, who rules in Samaria. He will be at Naboth's vineyard in Jezreel, claiming it for himself. Give him this message: 'This is what the LORD says: Wasn't it enough that you killed Naboth? Must you rob him, too? Because you have done this, dogs will lick your blood at the very place where they licked the blood of Naboth!'"

"So, my enemy, you have found me!" Ahab exclaimed to Elijah.

"Yes," Elijah answered, "I have come because you have sold yourself to what is evil in the LORD's sight. So now the LORD says, 'I will bring disaster on you and consume you. I will destroy every one of your male descendants, slave and free alike, anywhere in Israel! I am going to destroy your family as I did the family of Jeroboam son of Nebat and the family of Baasha son of Ahijah, for you have made me very angry and have led Israel into sin.'

And regarding Jezebel, the LORD says, 'Dogs will eat Jezebel's body at the plot of land in Jezreel. The members of Ahab's family who die in the city will be eaten by dogs, and those who die in the field will be eaten by vultures.'"

(No one else so completely sold himself to what was evil in the LORD's sight as Ahab did under the influence of his wife Jezebel. His worst outrage was worshiping idols just as the Amorites had done— the people whom the LORD had driven out from the land ahead of the Israelites.)

But when Ahab heard this message, he tore his clothing, dressed in burlap, and fasted. He even slept in burlap and went about in deep mourning.

Then another message from the LORD came to Elijah: "Do you see how Ahab has humbled himself before me? Because he has done this, I will not do what I promised during his lifetime. It will happen to his sons; I will destroy his dynasty."

As I finished reading this, I felt led to read it again. And then I almost heard Holy Spirit say, "Read it again." I was getting a little frustrated, but was obedient. And this time, I homed in on the part in parentheses:

(No one else so completely sold himself to what was evil in the LORD's sight as Ahab did under the influence of his wife Jezebel. His worst outrage was worshiping idols just as the Amorites had done—the people whom the LORD had driven out from the land ahead of the Israelites.)

It was as if the writer of the narrative I had been reading took a break to zero in on how horrible this King Ahab was. As if the writer of the text wanted you to know, unequivocally, this man was the pits. The scum of the earth. The lowest of the low. But when he heard Elijah's message, he seemed to repent by tearing his clothes, dressing in burlap, fasting, and mourning. And God recognized this and removed his consequence. His punishment. His death sentence. God showed him great mercy and grace because he had humbled himself.

As I came to these epiphanies and sat in awe of God's ability to forgive, I began to cry. And then I heard God's voice. "Leslie, do you see how horrible this man was? Do you see the evil he did and the evil he allowed to be done? But yet, I forgave him because he showed just a small turn toward me. Daughter, I am not up here with a hammer, ready to hit you in the head every time you make a mistake. I am up here desiring to shower down on you all the blessings I can muster. He was an evil king who worshiped other gods and completely rejected me. You have begged forgiveness for all your sins, and you have dedicated your life to me. Loved me. Worshiped me. Honored me. You are my daughter whom I wish to bless."

I was crying so hard I couldn't see. I turned over on my bed, laying there sobbing for quite a while. He had called me "daughter!" His daughter! My thoughts from the night before came rushing back. For almost 20 years I had only addressed Jesus. My prayers had been to Jesus. My praise had been to Jesus. My love had to been for Jesus. I was afraid of God.

Was it because I had internalized the Old Testament version of God? The God who brought judgment and punishments and had anger that could destroy someone in a second? Was this how I saw God? My dad's face immediately came to mind. This is exactly how I saw him also. Spanking me BEFORE we went somewhere "just in case you misbehave." Pulling my pants down to spank me when I was much too old for that kind of punishment. He knew that kind of punishment should never be carried out on a child because it's about shaming, not discipline. Punishing me if I didn't do a chore right. Had I projected all of my dad's behaviors onto God? I frequently taught my clients that we often wear the same glasses to look at God as we view our earthly fathers. Had I ignored my own advice and done exactly that?

Then remembering Jesus' words in John 14:11, "Believe me when I say that I am in the Father, and the Father is in me. The words I say to you I do not speak on my own authority. Rather it is the Father, living in me, who is doing His work."

Wow! Jesus came to show us the Father. He came so that we might know His character and His love for us. His grace and His mercy. His desire to have a relationship with us! This was all new territory for me, but I loved it! Crying even harder, I spoke out loud, "Oh, God, please forgive me! Please know I hear you and I am so grateful for how you love me! From now on you will be my Daddy and I am your daughter. Thank you. Thank you. Thank you! Thank you for your patience with this confused and misinformed woman. I get it now. And I will share this moment with anyone who will listen . . . because I know I am not alone.

***

That was the beginning of a whole new place in my faith walk. I had deprogrammed some serious junk, and reprogrammed with the truth. I began to look at things in a different way and to see people in a different light. My hunger to tell anyone I met all He had done for me was renewed and ready to be kindled. But I had some loose ends to tie up. I had to be free of the oppression that had kept me from seeing things clearly. And that was the next thing on my agenda.

20

A Light in the Darkness

"Fools are headstrong and do what they like; wise people take advice."
Proverb 12:15 The Message

I had to do a lot of planning to begin a course of healthy boundaries in my home. Boundaries that would protect all of us from any more abuse. I had made a covenant with God to make this marriage work, but so much of that covenant—so many of those promises made at the altar . . . "to have and to hold" and "to love and cherish from this day forward"—were already broken. There was no trust left. No love left . . . not even a little bit.

This ability to plan a new path for my family was the beautiful outcome of finally being free. I had spent many years in a tortured existence of self-blame and self-hatred. And this marriage had multiplied it.

So let me review a few things here before we move into my healthier life. The precursors that God used to heal my deepest hurts. I mentioned in the last chapter, I had 4 children. There had only been one blessing that came out of this marriage and that was my little girl, Rebekah. In all the darkness this man brought into my life, she was the only representation of light. My boys had always been my shining lights in my last disaster of a marriage, and they still were. But Rebekah was the product of this marriage, and she kept me afloat, and it certainly wasn't her job. I had prayed for a little girl with each pregnancy, as I guess every parent would like to experience both a son and a daughter. But God had always blessed me with boys. Three years into this marriage, at the age of 42—when I actually thought I was experiencing the woman's change of life—I became pregnant with my daughter. I was so thrilled, as were my boys.

137

And there was actually a very short period of time when I thought we might actually be able to live a normal life. But it wasn't to be.

Unfortunately, her birth only caused more division in the family, as her father was extremely biased towards her, and the boys felt it. There were already issues cropping up, like pornography, that when discovered, he blamed on the boys and then punished them—regardless of their pleas of innocence. And he was the guilty party.

He had a goal to get rid of my oldest boy because he viewed him as the "protector" and the only one who would stand up to him. Mike spoke about what he saw, and he saw a lot, and that upset the apple cart for my husband. He was eventually successful, kicking Mike out when none of the rest of us were home, and then telling the family that Mike had left of his own free will. We were all broken-hearted, and we didn't even know where Mike went. I didn't learn about this deception until much later, when Mike felt safe enough to tell me the whole truth.

There was constant nitpicking on the two remaining boys that apparently was at its worst when I was at work. But no one was talking. No one was telling me what was going on at home. I even suspected some of the behaviors I was seeing in the boys, and began taking them to a therapist, but they wouldn't tell him anything either. Then when I was taken out of work with an injury, there was still no transparency. I was on extended disability leave and decided to homeschool the kids. So, for a short time, it felt like things were better with them. But that was when he began his extramarital affairs. And until I discovered what he was doing, we all just had to put up with his increased verbal and emotional abuse. We all walked on eggshells.

And what was I doing? Falling deeper and deeper into a trauma response. I had fully reached the levels of freeze and fawn. The lies were endless, and the sickness was pervading.

Let me define this for you. What is a trauma response? There are 4 responses the human body experiences when faced with trauma—flight, fight, freeze and fawn. When we respond with aggression we exhibit the fight *response. If we run from the situation, we exhibit the* flight *response. If we feel we can't make decisions about things or become unable to respond in a crisis this may be the* freeze *response. And with complex PTSD we may also see the* fawn *response, which is avoiding conflict through people-pleasing. This serves as a coping-mechanism for the victim who will shut down their own needs, agree with the abuser to avoid conflict or further abuse, and/or seek their approval. This is a behavior that often begins in childhood as a stress response, and then through continued exposure to toxic relationships can create a cycle of codependence in adulthood. People who fawn will often be targeted by narcissists as easy prey.*

Some of the precursors that form this type of trauma response are things like bullying, domestic violence relationships, childhood abuse, and emotional/ physical abuse or neglect. The symptoms present themselves as a person who is constantly people-pleasing, an inability to recognize or even name what feelings they may be experiencing, appeasing the abuser to prevent more abuse, and poor boundaries or an inability to set boundaries.

As much as I hate to admit it, this is the horrific place where I had traveled. I didn't know what was wrong with me. All I knew was I had shut down and become a puppet, and was often not even able to take a shower, make a meal, or even get out of bed. My daughter had never known the mother I was to my boys. And my boys didn't recognize who I had become. I had only one goal: keep the peace at all cost. It was the only way I knew to survive. Only Jesus knew how to rescue me from this abyss I had entered. And He had guided me to the one counselor who was able to break open my shackles and lead me out of my prison. The freedom I felt was like breathing fresh air for the first time.

When I got to this new place of healing, I had to think about the kids and how my choices were going to affect their safety. I knew it would take some time to get my ducks in a row, and I began to prepare. I continued to work with my counselor and let the truth of Daddy's love for me sink in. And sink in deep. I would need all of that strength to make this break a possibility. The boys were old enough to make their own decisions, but Rebekah was young and if we separated, the thought of her spending time alone with him was a nightmare. So, I came up with a deal to offer him. If he attended *Every Man's Battle Conference Weekend,* and followed it with serious counseling, I would make every effort to work on the marriage as well. We had already tried marriage counseling with 3 different counselors, and his malignant narcissism was a plague each time. He was either extremely charismatic trying to win them to "his side." Or if any suggestion of accountability was thrown in his direction, he blew a fuse and refused to go back. I had worked hard on myself for the past several months, and had done a lot of work before I met him, so the ball was in his court.

I called some counselor friends of mine and was able to obtain a weekend for him, all expenses paid. All he had to do was go. So, I decided that night, I would present it to him. I also had plan B in place. If he didn't accept it, he had till the end of the month to move out.

I told the kids to stay in their rooms so Daddy and I could have a private conversation, but Rebekah stalled. I could tell something was heavy on her heart. "Are you going to make him leave?"

"Sweetheart, we will be discussing some things, but it isn't for you to worry about."

"Mom, you have said you would make him leave so many times and you never follow through. You need to keep your word." Wow! Another wake-up call from the mouth of one of my babes. Talk about a guilt trip. I silently sent up a prayer of grateful thanks for all Jesus had done for me, and then I addressed my daughter.

"Rebekah, I hope you can forgive Mommy for all the empty words she has promised and all the times you didn't feel safe. Those days are over. I promise." I kissed her and sent her upstairs. Guilt and shame were trying to raise their ugly heads, and I was not going to buy into it. I may have messed up in the past, but the future would look different from now on.

He would be arriving any minute, so I sent up some quick prayers of praise, and requests for strength. No sooner had I finished than I heard the front door open. He seemed to be in a pretty decent mood, *so here goes.*

"I was wondering if we could talk about some things before dinner."

Stone faced. No emotion. "OK. What is it now?"

"I have been feeling disrespected when I try to talk to you about our relationship. When I try to share my feelings, it seems we end up discussing how everything affects you, and I don't feel like I am being heard."

Smirk followed by eye roll. "Of course, just make me out to be the bad guy. OK, here it is! I am the bad guy. I don't ever listen to anything you say. I am a jerk. A terrible person! Are you happy now?" *Case in point.*

"We need to come to some common ground if we are going to continue to live together. I have some ideas I think could be a good starting point, so the kids and I feel safe."

Placating face. Smirk. "Oh, YOU have some ideas! And somehow it's me that makes you all feel unsafe?" *Arms thrown up in the air. Very exaggerated movements.* "Well, since your ideas are always so brilliant, and nothing I suggest has any merit, let's hear them." Goes to the kitchen and gets a soda.

My heartbeat is increasing. Stomach churning. Stay calm, Leslie. You can do this. "I talked to a friend of mine who was able to get an all-expenses paid *Every Man's Battle Weekend* for you. And I would like you to attend it, and then follow up with some weekly counseling." *There. Got it out.*

"What in the hell is *Every Man's Battle Weekend?*" *Eye roll and head shake.*

"It's a weekend for men who are addicted to pornography and the consequential acting out of their addiction by having affairs and other things, like phone sex and going to stripper bars. They help men understand why they do it, and even offer an accountability partner so they can overcome it."

Dramatic guffaws, then points his finger in my face. "I will not humiliate myself for you by attending something that stupid. I have no problems. You are the one with the problems. Look at you! Why wouldn't I look elsewhere?" *Smirks and flops in the chair.*

Weird. No pain felt by that comment. And my resolve was still strong. "OK. That's your choice. But if you don't go, you have 30 days to get out of this house. And you won't be coming back." *No shaking. No voice tremors. No backing down. I was proud of me!*

"Fine. I will get out. I won't humiliate myself anymore by staying here." He then got up, went into the bedroom, and went to bed.

I decided to sleep in the guest room, so I got my pajamas from our bedroom, shut the door and called the kids for dinner. After everyone sat down to eat and we had said grace, I took a few deep breaths. "Guys, your dad is going to move out of the house at the end of the month. We both feel this is the best thing for the family. I don't have any answers as to what this may look like going forward, but that's where things are now."

No one said a word, and then Matthew asked if I would pass the chicken. Nothing else was said. No arguments. No questions.

Over the next few weeks, Rebekah repeatedly asked me if I was really going to keep my word this time. Every time she did, it made me feel terrible that I had ever let her down. I repeatedly assured her nothing would change my mind. This was brought to a head the following night. I needed to go to the grocery store, and she did not want to go with me, so I asked her if she was okay to stay home with her dad. She agreed and I assumed all was well.

When I came in with the groceries, Rebekah followed me into the kitchen, and she was crying. I hunkered down and asked her what had happened, and she said our Golden Retriever, Sandy, had tried to get close to him and had crawled behind his legs. He had apparently yelled and then pounded her in the back with his fist as hard as he could. She said Sandy had yelped and then just laid there. "I was afraid she was dead, Mom!"

I pulled her close and hugged her tight. "I am so sorry, baby." I then called Sandy, and she came to me right away, and seemed to be ok. I hugged her, too. "How about if Sandy sleeps with you tonight? Would you like that?"

Rebekah pulled back her head and looked me dead in the eyes. "Yes, I would, but Mom don't you dare not kick him out of here. Promise me."

I looked into her eyes and felt the pain I saw there. "Two days, baby. Just two more days."

That time passed quickly, and as he was packing and taking his stuff out, Rebekah and I watched TV and never even acknowledged him. It was a wonderful day for both of us.

***

One year later, he filed for divorce. He had been living with another woman most of that time, but I had never felt God give me the okay to file myself. I had plenty of grounds, but God encouraged me to pray. Pray for his repentance. Pray for his heart. Pray for his soul. And I did. Faithfully. But to no avail. I received the papers with a sigh of relief. It will finally be over. The 15-year nightmare was coming to an end. My only fear was I had no way to keep him from visitation with Rebekah. I had to let her go with him every other weekend, and every time she did, I felt like I could hardly take a deep breath until she was back in my arms again.

The door did not completely shut for a few more years. There is always a source of some drama or passive aggressive behavior when you deal with a narcissist. The boys visited him on occasion until he refused to go to David's wedding and then he was cut off for good in the boys' lives. Rebekah became disillusioned with him after catching him cheating on the girl he was living with, but she still had to see him on his assigned weekends. She was within a year of being able to make her own decision about those, and I counted the days. So, when he showed up at her school the following year, disrupted her class, made threats toward me, and then flattened her tires, she was done. She was afraid and wanted to get a protective order. She knew he owned an unregistered gun, since they had gone target shooting together, and she was scared for herself . . . and me. But as always, he turned on the charisma in court for the judge and the judge bought his lies. And it was the last time Rebekah saw him. And, finally, the door shut for me.

After that chapter closed, I wondered what my life was going to look like going forward. I had not experienced a life free of adrenaline rushes, cortisol dumps and eggshell walking since I had been a single mom the first time. Following the work I had done with my counselor, I knew all things were being made new. It had taken a lot of time, but I felt in my spirit God was not done with me yet. What would the next steps look like? What plans did He have for me? It was a mystery, but it was finally a mystery I didn't have to fear.

21

Horizons

Acclimating to a life free of anxiety can actually be a bit unnerving. When the body is accustomed to the surge of adrenaline, cortisol, and epinephrine on a daily basis, the absence of them can make you feel off. Abnormal. Uncomfortable. Ironically, it's almost anxiety provoking because you don't understand why you are feeling so different. As I became more accustomed to this new sensation, I noticed I was feeling better. I realized the hormones that had been shut down from the constant stress—endorphins, dopamine, serotonin, and oxytocin—were now being released into my system. I was sleeping better, eating less, and RESTING. This was something I almost never experienced as a child or as an adult. I distinctly recall my counselor asking me how I have been feeling since my husband had moved out. It took no time for me to answer. "I feel like I am smiling all the time now."

And it was true. I smiled at the people in the store. At the doctor's office. At church. Everywhere I went, I smiled. It actually made me wonder what my face looked like before. I even found myself complimenting people on something they were wearing, or how attractive they looked. It felt like I was experiencing a whole new life. I felt restless. I felt apprehensive. I felt anticipatory and eager. But I didn't know what was around the corner. The only thing I did know was it would be good. Because Daddy was a good, good Father.

I began to pray about where God wanted me. The only one of my kids still at home was Rebekah. Mike had gotten married, and David and Matthew were in college. I was open to whatever He suggested, I just needed to hear His voice. For the first time in my life, I felt confident that whatever He placed in my path, He would also equip me to do it.

Out of the blue, I received a notice from our local community college about a teaching position. It was to train CNA's. I applied and found it had already been filled but the advisor I spoke with asked if I had other training I could utilize to teach a non-credit community class. I went home that night and thought about areas I had great interest in and those I had studied. I had taken 3 classes at our church about religions other than Christianity, and how they differed from it. I had really enjoyed those classes, so, after much prayer, I called the advisor and asked if they would be interested in a class on World Religions. She was all for it. She asked me to develop a curriculum and submit it to her, and she would let me know a start date.

As I worked on the curriculum, I became aware of how very much I enjoyed digging even deeper into religious origins, and especially the origins of my own faith. By the end of my second semester of teaching, I realized this was something that went deeper than just enjoyment. This was a *passion*. I continued to pursue God's leading as to where He wanted me. Was all of this reflection I was doing somehow the foundation of an answer to that question?

Then one evening as I was perusing the history of Judaism, a light bulb went off. "Is this where you want me, Daddy? Going back to school? Studying religion?" An immediate response came.

"Yes, daughter, this is where I want you. I want you to pursue going back to school. And I want you to go to Bible college."

I was grateful for such a clear answer, but scared at the same time. I was 54 years old. That's a little over the hill to be earning a new college degree. But, as I said earlier, if He was leading me, He would equip me. I called my church and made an appointment with my pastor to ask him about his recommendations, and he told me about Nazarene Bible College. It was a school that actually existed to help older people pursue their degree to become a pastor. But they also had other curricula, including counseling. Well, I couldn't have heard any better news than that!

I prayed hard and filled out the application the next day. I received an immediate response requesting me to send my transcripts, informing me an answer would be forthcoming. I was so excited! I chose to keep everything to myself until I had an answer. That evening, I was very contemplative about if I truly wanted to be a pastor. I had no desire to preach, but I would love to teach about God's Word. I thoroughly enjoyed the Bible studies I attended, in and out of church, and those I had taught in my singles group. I especially loved the Old Testament. Pastor had also mentioned the counseling curriculum that led to a degree. I had already been teaching psychoeducational classes and doing supervision in a behavioral health unit, so this would expand my knowledge base, and open more doors for me going forward. I was barely able to sleep that night.

Weeks passed. I heard nothing from the school. I worried my barely-above-average- grades from my last college had become a roadblock. I wondered if I had really heard God's voice leading me. And behind that, I worried about how I was going to support my daughter and our home without a full-time job. And how was that going to look if I was in school full-time? Too many worries. I had to leave all of this in Daddy's hands. If I had missed His leading, He would re-direct. I had to be patient.

The answer came the next day. The email congratulated me . . . and I was in! I will be starting classes in two weeks. The excitement I felt was off the chart. I then found that I could continue teaching at the college, so all I needed was another part-time job as an adjunct to it. Something to give me enough time to study and still be a mom. God had not failed me yet, so I had to trust, once again. The second part-time job came later that week when a fellow nurse told me about temporary employment giving flu shots at a local store. I could pick my own hours, and the pay was excellent! I filled out the application and was hired immediately. I started the following week, so I would have the newness of it under my belt before I started classes. God had done it again.

***

Bible College was so much more than just an education. I loved my counseling classes. All that I had already learned as a psychiatric nurse was being layered with so much more about the counseling realm. I ate it up. And even more than those classes, I loved studying, in detail, God's Word and the historical background of my faith. The spiritual growth I was experiencing was immense, but I knew there was so much more to learn. All the attempts my father had made to discredit the Bible were now being evaporated in truth. God's truth. And it made my heart feel like it was on fire. Those days at Nazarene Bible College were some of my best memories. One of the coolest was when I had to write a personal Life Mission Statement. It poured out of me because it represented everything I had missed in my life . . . and longed for. This is what I wrote:

I want to use my God-given skills to help people
learn to communicate truth to each other, without fear,
relinquishing misperceptions of self and others,
and to find their identity in Christ alone.

***

A lot happened over the next two years. Some good. Some challenges. But I persevered in school and made straight A's. I got one B+ in Theology, and it felt like a fail—but only temporarily. There was a good reason. For the last six months I had traveled back and forth to see my very best friend of 40 years, Camelia. Her cancer had been misdiagnosed, and by the time they finally corrected it, she was terminal. It was my Theology class that felt the brunt of it. I asked for grace on a few of my papers, but rules are rules. I lost her in December. I couldn't even attend her funeral because of a snowstorm. It created a large vacuum in my life. She and I had been through much together. And she was the last connection I had to my old life.

My son, David, was also supposed to graduate the same year I was, but he changed his major at the last minute, and was delayed a year. So, we planned his wedding instead. That was to be in Chicago, and my graduation in Colorado. My dad and Rebekah attended my ceremony and then we flew to Chicago to be part of David's wedding. Though I excused my boys' absence at my graduation as conflicting with the time they needed to be preparing for the wedding plans in Chicago, I soon realized this may have been my first indication of some leftover issues between my sons and me. Were they suffering their own trauma bonds from all we had experienced? Was I going to be an ugly reminder of all we had been through? Or were they possibly holding me accountable for my mental and emotional absence during that time? And it wasn't just the boys. I was feeling it with my daughter, too. At the time, I didn't know where it would lead. Only time would tell.

22

A New Creation

I prayed about how to close this journey through my life. How to express in words the extent of healing Jesus has done in it. The average person may look at me and see a woman who is in the winter of her life, and who doesn't possess the riches or abundance of many others who are my age. I won't lie and pretend I had a good financial planner that guaranteed a comfortable retirement. That may very well be the way the world would assess my situation. And there are others who may look at me and wonder what I have actually accomplished in my life. And that's where I would ask them to sit down and encourage them to share with me what "success" looks like to them.

Because success for me is not about having everything I want, but being blessed with everything I need. It's about having a sound mind, and the gifts of wisdom and discernment from on High. It's about knowing what the "peace that surpasses man's understanding" actually feels like. It's about remembering I was a lost soul who felt she had no purpose, no future, and no hope . . . and was granted mercy and grace. A person who was miraculously rescued from that very dark existence. It's knowing God has blessed me with the ability to view people through His eyes—without judgment and without prejudice—and see into their pain . . . and then help Him lead them out. And there is nothing on the planet more rewarding and fulfilling than that.

As I came to the place of closing *The Rescue of an Orphan,* I looked back at my roots. The ones I shared in *The Making of an Orphan.* The family roots. The roots that had no fertile ground. The roots that were formed out of trauma. The generational trauma that has been present for decades. And the very real possibility that I may have passed that trauma onto my own children. And that hurts. It hurts at a level I can't put into words.

But as I said in *The Making of an Orphan,* the buck stops here. I have done the hard work. The pages of this book attest to it. And I can only pray that my children, who are all young adults now, will open their hearts to the same healing. One of them has. He is on the road to healing. I can only pray, the others will do the same, and recognize that Jesus is always pursuing them. Always loving them. Always offering grace, mercy . . . and restoration. And my daily prayer is that they, too, will surrender to His rescue.

So, this is the end of my story. My degree in Counseling for Christian Ministries has not been lucrative in the way of finances, but it has been priceless in the way it has allowed me to help many who trudge through their life challenges. The Scripture God gave me, all those years ago, in 2 Corinthians, has proved itself true. God has continuously brought people into my life who have walked, or are walking, the roads I have. Needing the same truth He provided for me. The same care He provided for me. And seeking the same hope that can only be found at the foot of a cross where our Savior died . . . so we can be free.

The Savior, who tenderly held a little girl, scared and confused, in His arms and led her out of her 33-year abyss.

The Savior, who touched the arm of a woman who was praying for a miracle at the birth of her baby, and revealed Himself to her with the words, "Trust me."

The Savior, who, though she didn't know Him yet, stepped in—supernaturally—to rescue a young 15-year-old from the violent acts of a motorcycle gang.

This is the Savior of whom I speak. The One who did these things for me.
And He will do them for you.
He is my Way. He is my Truth. He is my Life. He is my Jesus. He sought me.
He rescued me. He forgave me. He healed me.
And He redeemed me.
And He never stopped working on me until I had become *that* person.
Not the person the world had created.
But the person our Daddy created me to be.

Epilogue

I t all began with a little girl named Karin, the young Leslie, who just wanted to be loved and was unaware of what her future held. It was uncertain if she was safe. Didn't know there was the option of unconditional love or that it even existed. She was oblivious to the possibility of being rescued. Subconsciously, she longed for it, but knew only trepidation, anxiety, and fear in her little heart and mind. What she lived was all she knew of "normal." And, oh my, it was so far from normal.

As I scanned back through my manuscript of *The Making of an Orphan*, I paused at a place that was especially tender. A place in my memory that exemplified the life I led as a little child. In Wheaton, sitting in front of the TV, by herself, watching Charlie Brown's Christmas. She was feeling something but didn't know what it was. I decided to join her. She was sitting on the floor in front of the TV. The room was a bit chilly, but it felt all the colder because she was completely alone.

"Do you mind if I sit with you, Karin?"

She looks a bit taken aback, and then smiles, "Sure! I love this show! It only comes on at Christmas and it's so good! Have you seen it?"

I get down on the floor next to her, and sit cross-legged like she is. "Yes, Karin, it's one of my favorites, too. I especially like the part when Linus talks about what Christmas really is. Do you like that part?"

"I love that part! It always gives me a funny feeling in my tummy. But it's a good feeling!"

My heart skips a beat as I feel that in my own gut. "Why are you sitting here alone? Wouldn't it be more fun to watch this with your parents?"

"Yes, that would be nice, but they are always busy. Dad works all the time, and so he is in his office, and Mom always has something to do around the house. So, they tell me to watch TV so I will be out of their way."

She looks down at her hands. And as she does, I experience the same empty pit I know she is feeling . . . and often felt. She looks up at the TV, as the commercial ends, where Charlie Brown has gathered all the kids for practice.

We watch together in silence as Charlie becomes frustrated with the group not listening to his direction, and then leaves with Linus to get a Christmas tree for the play. Another commercial. She looks at me smiling, "That good part is getting ready to come on! You know the part we both like!" I nod and my heart skips more beats as I feel her excitement.

The commercial ends, and the show commences. Charlie brings the tree in, and most of the needles seem to fall off as he places it on the piano. Everyone laughs at him, and he looks down sadly and says to Linus, "I guess you were right Linus. I shouldn't have picked this little tree. Everything I do turns into a disaster. I guess I really don't know what Christmas is all about." He looks up at the ceiling and asks loudly, "Isn't there anyone who knows what Christmas is all about?"

Karin looks at me and says, "Here it is!" And I feel her heartbeat increase and her little stomach jump, as she listens to Linus sharing the story of the birth of Jesus. We watch together as Linus finishes his narrative, and then tells Charlie, "That's what Christmas is all about, Charlie Brown." Then we watch as all the kids join him to decorate the tree and sing the closing song. I see her folding her little hands, and feel the inner peace she is feeling.

"Wasn't that great? I just love that show. Thank you for watching it with me. Who are you anyways?"

I chuckle at her use of "anyways" knowing Dad would certainly have promptly corrected her every time she did it. "My name is Leslie, and I came here tonight to keep you company while you watched this, because I knew how lonely you felt."

She smiles. "That's my first name!"

I smile and nod, and then she suddenly looks confused, and I knew it was time. "Karin, this may sound confusing, but I am you—just all grown up. And I especially wanted to meet you here tonight to share with you the real meaning of Linus' words. Why do you think you felt a special way whenever you hear the part Linus shares?"

She seems contemplative, looks down, and then back at me. "I don't know. I just feel it in my stomach. It's like the feeling I get when I am excited about something good."

I smile at my little self and distinctly remember how hard it was to explain that feeling. Especially because it happened so infrequently. I touch her shoulder, and encourage her to sit on my lap. I snuggle her as she settles in. "Do you remember when Linus said the angel of the Lord told the shepherds that a Savior had been born unto them? Do you know what a Savior is?"

Karin looks bewildered, and then brightens. "Yes! Ms. Clara used to tell us in Sunday School about Jesus being a Savior. But I don't really know what that means."

I feel the warmth of tears as they begin forming in my eyes. The innocence of this little girl makes me want to hug her so tightly with all the love she so desperately needs. The attachment to another human who finds her to be the perfect little princess she was created to be. I mourn for the years I know she will have to wait to realize the truth I was about to tell her. And the deep desire to save her from all she would have to experience . . . until that great and wonderful day arrives in her life, and everything she knows will be turned upside down. But for now, I will settle on giving her the hope that we will discover together . . . many years from now.

"Karin, a Savior is someone who rescues you. Rescues you from many terrible things. He only asks that you believe that He is the only One who can. The only One who can forgive your sins and promise you everlasting life with Him in Heaven. He wants you to believe He died for you on the cross, so that you could experience the grace and mercy of a life led by Him. And that offer He makes is life changing! Because He becomes the Lord of your life, and begins to take away all the hurt and pain you have experienced, and replaces it with His love. A love that will never leave or forsake you. A love that fills you with hope and the promise of better things. And that feeling you get in your tummy is the desire to meet Him. The desire God created within you to have a personal relationship with Him.

"Karin, I have come here to tell you about an incredible rescue that will happen to you much later in life, at a time when you will feel hopeless and believe there is no possible way out of the situation you are in. But there will be. And His name is Jesus. He rescues us from every sad moment. And every tear we have ever cried, He has collected and saved in a bottle. He loves us that much.

"And I will write a book about us. All our troubles. All our insecurities. All our pain. And I will finally tell the story of your life, and you will be freed from the bondage of never feeling loved. And you will experience the freedom of knowing a Savior who loved you so much, He never stopped chasing after you. And I will talk about the beauty of how that completely changed our lives, as His love overpowered all the evil, hurt and pain we had experienced. And you will finally be free. And with your freedom, will come my freedom. The freedom to become the person God created me to be."

I realize as I finish talking how very tight Karin is hugging me. And that feeling in my gut, that we shared, was very present. That pleasant and beautiful feeling of something good happening. And then I realize I am sitting alone, at home, and typing on my computer . . .

⁎

Healing the little person inside each of us is a journey. Integration with your younger— very damaged, and now healed—former self is not an easy road. It's a road of much pain. Reliving the traumas of your life can be like driving on the Autobahn at 500 mph with no brakes. Pulse racing. Heart pounding out of your chest. Or it can feel like your whole body is completely asleep, but you know you aren't because your eyes are wide open. Numb. Mindless. Thoughts wondering. Or it can feel like running as fast as you can in the opposite direction of the pain because you just KNOW you can't feel that intensity even one more time.

But here is the catch. If you don't face it, you ARE living it every day. You just find ways to numb it. And there are so many ways. Alcohol, drugs, gambling, food, relationships, shopping, video games, pornography, exercise, and, well, the list goes on . . . and on . . . and on. Then we finally reach a place in our older age where our brain can't stuff it down any longer, and we begin to act out the pain. And we find new ways to numb it. This is often where "mid-life crises" happen. Whatever it is—it's not going to be pretty . . . or healthy.

I say all that to say this: As painful as you think healing might be, it's nowhere near as bad as it will be if you wait. And the good news? You have a Savior who wants to help you walk through it. To hold you through the tears. To remind you how special you are to Him.

To rescue you . . .

END

References

Holy Bible, New International Version. (2011). Zondervan. (Original work published 1973). Boyce, P. (2023). *Light for the Journey through Dry Bone Valley.* Renown.

Carnes, P. (1997). *The Betrayal Bond: Breaking free of exploitive relationships.* Deerfield Beach, FL: Health Communications, Inc.

Chbosky, S. (1999). *The Perks of Being a Wallflower.* New York, NY: Pocket Books.

Hemfelt, R., Minirth, F., Meier, P. (1989). *Love is a Choice.* Nashville, TN: Thomas Nelson.

Keffer, S. (2018). *Intimate Deception: Healing the wounds of sexual betrayal.* Grand Rapids, MI: Revell.

Resources

An Autobiography in Five Chapters
by Portia Nelson

Chapter 1
I walk down the street.
There is a deep hole in the sidewalk.
I fall in. I am lost . . . I am helpless.
It isn't my fault.
It takes forever to find a way out.

Chapter 2
I walk down the same street.
There is a deep hole in the sidewalk.
I pretend I don't see it. I fall in again.
I can't believe I am in the same place.
But it isn't my fault.
It still takes a long time to get out.

Chapter 3
I walk down the same street.
There is a deep hole in the sidewalk.
I see it is there.
I fall in . . . it's a habit . . . but my eyes are open.
I know where I am. It is my fault.
I get out immediately.

Chapter 4
I walk down the same street.
There is a deep hole in the sidewalk.
I walk around it.

Chapter 5
I walk down a different street.

Abortion Signs and Symptoms

How Do You Know You Need Healing?

Are you reluctant to talk about the abortion?

Do you find you avoid attending baby showers or being around babies?

Are you experiencing depression or feelings of unworthiness?

Do you feel guilt, anger, shame or sorrow in relation to your abortion?

Are you experiencing difficulty in building or maintaining close relationships?

Have you noticed a pattern of destructive behaviors in your life?

Are you struggling with an eating disorder or food addiction?

Do you have feelings of bitterness, anger or resentment toward those involved in your abortion?

Are you using drugs or alcohol in order to cope?

Do you avoid sexual intimacy or struggle with promiscuity?

Do you have nightmares, dreams or flashbacks related to the abortion?

Does the anniversary month of the abortion OR your due date disrupt your life each year?

If you have other children, do you find you have difficulty attaching to them OR are afraid of them being out of your sight?

If you answered "yes" to any of these questions,
you could benefit from visiting this site:
www.silentnomoreawareness.org
Help is available!

About the Author

eslie T. Dean has been a registered nurse for 43 years. She has served as a Behavioral Health Counselor, Psychiatric Nurse Manager, and Pastoral Counselor. In 2012, Leslie graduated from Nazarene Bible College with honors, having earned her degree in Counseling for Christian Ministries. More recently she has been certified as a Professional Christian Life Coach and Certified Trauma-Informed Care Coach. She has counseled victims of abuse, codependency, and abortion for over thirty years.

Her first book, *Forgiven Much*, a novel about the life of Mary Magdalene, has experienced continued success, especially since the popularity of the TV show *The Chosen*. It has also been popular in counseling centers and Pregnancy Resource Centers across the country, helping women find hope at the foot of the cross. Her second book, *The Making of an Orphan*, has sustained reviews offering the accounts from numerous people who have been helped by her message, and who are looking forward to the sequel, *The Rescue of an Orphan*.

Through continued study and healing in her own life, she has discovered the plague that intergenerational trauma passes on to families. She has learned that understanding the impact it has on the lives of each family member can begin the process of healing and forgiveness. Because of her personal experience in these areas, and through her many contacts, she has found that an epidemic number of people have experienced some form of abuse in their childhood. Sadly, many don't realize the long-term cost abuse and trauma have on their lives and the resulting effect it has on the choices they make as adults. Consequently, they often suffer with poor self-image, depression, substance abuse, relational dysfunction, and worse, the generational passing of the trauma baton.

Ms. Dean is also a conference leader and presents workshops where people find help and hope to understand how their past does not have to define their future. She has also served since 2009 as the Regional Coordinator in Maryland and Delaware for the *Silent No More Awareness Campaign*. Leslie has been instrumental in helping educate and mobilize people in both states to speak out about their abortion pain. For seven years she served as the nurse manager in a Maryland pregnancy center, performing ultrasounds on their patients, until she retired in 2023. In 2022, she joined forces with four other passionate, pro-life people to form a Board of Directors to birth a brand-new pregnancy care clinic in Seaford, DE, **Her Care Clinic**. She continues to enjoy assisting with ultrasounds for their clients.

www.ingramcontent.com/pod-product-compliance
Lightning Source LLC
Chambersburg PA
CBHW061258120726
48001CB00001B/353